FANTASTIC
Paper Airplanes

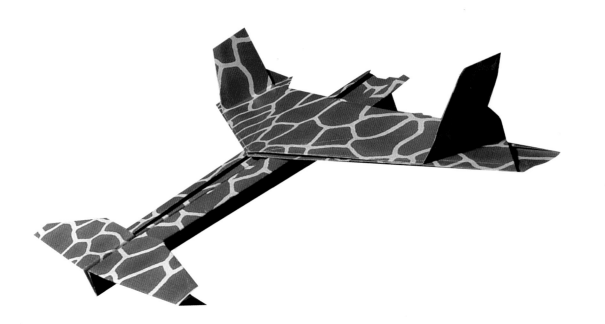

JACK BOTERMANS

FANTASTIC
Paper Airplanes

TEXT BY HELEEN TICHLER

Sterling Publishing Co., Inc.
New York

Models conceived and illustrated by Jack Botermans, Netherlands
Design and photography by Jack Botermans, Netherlands
Text by Heleen Tichler, Netherlands
Translation by Deborah Ogle, UK/USA
Edited by Claire Bazinet

NOTE: All parties involved in the preparation of this book must point out that while every care has been taken with the preparation of the instructions for folding and flying the models presented in this book, they will not be liable for any loss or damage of whatever kind suffered by or inflicted upon any person, creature, or property whether involved in folding and/or flying the models or not.

Library of Congress Cataloging-in-Publication Data Available

10 9 8 7 6 5 4 3 2

© 2003 by Sterling Publishing Co., Inc.
© 2002 by Bookman International bv, Netherlands,
and Jack Botermans, Netherlands.
Originally published in the Dutch language
under the title *Vliegen Met Papier.*
Published in paperback 2004 by
Sterling Publishing Co., Inc.
387 Park Avenue South, New York, NY 10016
Distributed in Canada by Sterling Publishing
C/o Canadian Manda Group, 165 Dufferin Street,
Toronto, Ontario, Canada M6K 3H6
Distributed in Great Britain and Europe by Chris Lloyd at Orca Book
Services, Stanley House, Fleets Lane, Poole BH15 3AJ, England
Distributed in Australia by Capricorn Link (Australia) Pty. Ltd.
P.O. Box 704, Windsor, NSW 2756, Australia

Printed in China
All rights reserved

Sterling ISBN 1-4027-0874-2
            (hardcover)
            1-4027-1149-2
            (paperback)

It's always difficult at first.

For information about custom editions, special sales, premium and corporate purchases, please contact Sterling Special Sales Department at 800-805-5489 or specialsales@sterlingpub.com.

CONTENTS

This bomber introduced the Euro bank notes in 2002.

Paper planes: just for kids, or an expression of the unfulfilled dreams of youth? For years, that was how people saw it, and those who took paper airplanes seriously were often ridiculed. A story is told of a well-known professor who idly made a paper airplane out of the program during a boring evening at the theatre. He impulsively let it fly, and it immediately attracted more attention than the action on the stage.

The turning point in paper airplanes becoming a respectable hobby came with a competition in *Scientific American* magazine. The first Inter-national Airplane Competition was announced on December 12, 1966, with a full-page ad in the *New York Times*: the inspiration being the new Lockheed-Boeing supersonic aircraft design the Concorde, certainly reminiscent of the old and familiar craft made from a sheet of paper. The response was enormous and, just as *Scientific American* suspected, there were rather more talented aircraft enthusiasts around than most people imagined.

Certainly, many devotees started by trying their hands at countless paper planes, at one time or another, from paper torn from school exercise books or color magazines. These craft, either clumsily or carefully folded, flew through the air to make their first of many smooth—or rough—landings. The old childhood model was definitely a favorite, but it looked rather awkward. So, soon another student would make a better one—one that was graceful and attractive in the air.

Another popular model is often crafted during a boring afternoon at the office. An irritating memo from the boss is folded eight times, then the glorious, satisfying result, a sweeping glide—the illusion of being in control, of the sky at least. Of course, it only lasts a few moments, and then the day's routine is reluctantly resumed.

But the paper plane is not a schooltime or business world discovery. Leonardo da Vinci, one of the first in a long line of aircraft inventors, experimented with planes made of parchment. And just think, if the Montgolfier brothers hadn't casually hung a paper bag up over a wood fire, the discovery of the hot air balloon would, in the course of time, probably have fallen eventually to someone else.

Paper has always been a fine medium to "fly like a bird." That dream continues, but the advent of jumbo jets and the Concorde has added weight. Like driving steam trains, now being a jet pilot means building replicas of airplanes, but what use is a plane too heavy to fly?

A noisy radio-controlled model made of balsa wood and glue can fly, but after working on it every Sunday afternoon for months, it might simply set itself on a quick course to self-destruction. Despite all the clever engineering, striving for an exact copy can often result in disappointment and disillusionment.

Far more rewarding is the plane quickly but carefully fashioned from paper. It glides through the air from the palm of the hand, hovering a while and causing no disturbing noise. No greasy hands or sticky fingers mar the fun. Paper planes are not dangerous and require nothing more than ingenuity, patience, and perseverance. They can fly indoors or out, in virtually any conditions—even a sultry summer evening can produce good results. A final piece of advice—put your name and address on the model in case of a spectacular maiden flight!

As you begin, folding paper planes may appear to be simple to do. Be assured, however, that many prototypes will end up making an untimely landing in the wastepaper basket, but persevere. The satisfaction of discovering that something as complicated as an F-16 can be made out of a simple piece of paper is priceless. And what's to prevent you from organizing an air show, designing all the models and painting them in your own colors? No special tools are needed: just two hands, patience, and the basic instructions you'll find here.

Paper Flight, a way to send airmail.

The principal tools for folding paper models are your own two hands. In some cases additional items may be needed but most are normally available in the home. Making successful aircraft involves conscientious practice and a detailed study of the diagrams. If something isn't immediately clear to you, examine the appropriate diagram carefully, make one or two practice folds, and the approach will quickly become apparent. Patience is absolutely essential.

GENERAL

Work on a clean surface. The basic material for crafting paper airplanes is, of course, paper. The weight used will depend on the size of the finished model. Models 4 to 8 inches (10 to 20 cm) require 16 lb. (60g) paper. The models shown in this book never call for paper heavier than 20 lb (80g); the approximate weight of average bond typing paper. Complex folding patterns call for a thinner paper, perhaps as fine as cigarette paper, but to do these requires experience. Generally, the larger the model the thicker the paper, but you can always experiment. Before attempting a model, always study the step-by-step diagrams carefully. In fact, the diagrams and photographs of the models will probably reveal more than any written explanation could. To make sharp, clean edges you may want to score the lines; you do this by scratching a straight line where the fold should be, using a scissors blade. It can be done with a knife but only on thick paper, or you risk cutting through the sheet. Some folds necessitate a "double crease," made by folding the paper backward and forward on the same line to achieve a flexible "hinge." In addition, there is the "inverted fold," shown and explained here.

READING THE DIAGRAMS

Dotted line: make the fold here, or make a double crease by folding backward and forward along the dotted line.
Solid line: the position of an existing fold or cut.
Scissors: cut along the line indicated.
Inverted fold: first fold the paper backward and forward along the dotted line, then push the top point inward as shown by the arrow; good sharp folds will make it easier.
Thunderbolt arrow: first make an inward and then an outward fold.
Overall, if you follow the direction of the arrows accurately, you can't go wrong.

TOOLS

The few you use must be good ones. You will need a sharp pair of scissors, preferably smaller ones, such as haircutting scissors; a soft-leaded pencil (to mark down measurements and be able to erase them later); a craft knife (the kind with a continuous blade and an end that can be snapped off once it becomes dull); paints and paintbrushes (poster paints are best as they won't dampen the model too much); paper glue; a stapler to fasten parts of the models together (cellophane or other tape, or glue are other possibilities); a ruler for measuring and to help make straight folds.

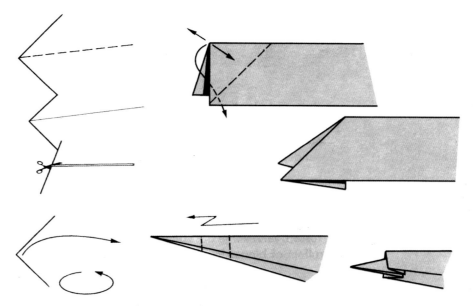

FANTASY FLYERS

This section includes a number of basic models, each one unique and providing plenty of scope for your imagination. In fact, the models are imaginary; that is, they bear no resemblance to any actual airplane design. Once you master the techniques used here, therefore, you can feel free to alter the designs to your own specifications.

You may decide to build an original Starfighter, delta wings and all, or imaginatively deliver a special message—"air" mail.

The first thing a carpenter learns is how to pound a nail into wood. In the case of paper aircraft, the first thing to learn is the art of folding paper: how, where, and in which direction to fold is clearly explained here with the help of diagrams. These make-believe models are designed to provide you with working methods and folding skills as thoroughly as possible, rather than concentrate on high-performance flights.

Eleven designs are included in this section. Some are easy to do—to help develop your command of the techniques—while others are more difficult. Try them all, experimenting by combining different designs. But make sure you have plenty of paper!

BASIC MODEL

Everyone has had experience with this model at some time. It's the one often launched at unsuspecting teachers while they write at the blackboard. The model is quickly and easily made from a sheet of paper 8 × 12 inches (20 × 30cm). The one shown here looks somewhat like a rocket. This is a good time to develop your own ideas and try to improve on this simple design. You may, for example, decide to glue on the wings of the Wright Flyer on page 16. The directions tell you to use a staple but you could glue it instead, making the model stronger and more stable. The rudders are folded and bent to enable the plane to perform differing flight patterns, as the instructions explain.

*An airplane with a history—
it has been aimed at many unsuspecting teachers.*

3 Again fold the two sides in to the center fold.

4 Make a double crease in the wing tips, along the dotted lines, and leave flat. Fold the models in half backward, along the dotted center line.

5 Staple (or glue) the underside of the fuselage together as indicated. Make a double crease in the tail as shown, and push the fold up through the rear of the fuselage to form a stabilizer. Finally, fold the wing tips up to loop-the-loop, down for dives, and one up one down for spiral dives.

1 Take a sheet of paper 8 × 12 inches (20 × 30 cm) and fold it in half lengthwise. Open it out flat and fold in the two corners, as shown by the dotted line.

2 Fold the two sides along the dotted lines, toward the center fold.

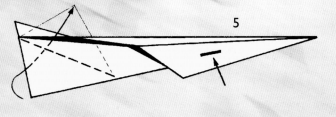

Be prepared for unscheduled flights
from this small tough aerobat.

This is an original cross between a French Mirage Jet and an African Zebra. We call it "Speedy Zebra" because it is a fast and cunning flyer with a tendency to set off suddenly in new and unexpected directions.
It's an easy model to fold so you can easily make a number of them at one time. Why not assemble a whole squadron, give them names or numbers, and set them aloft en mass?

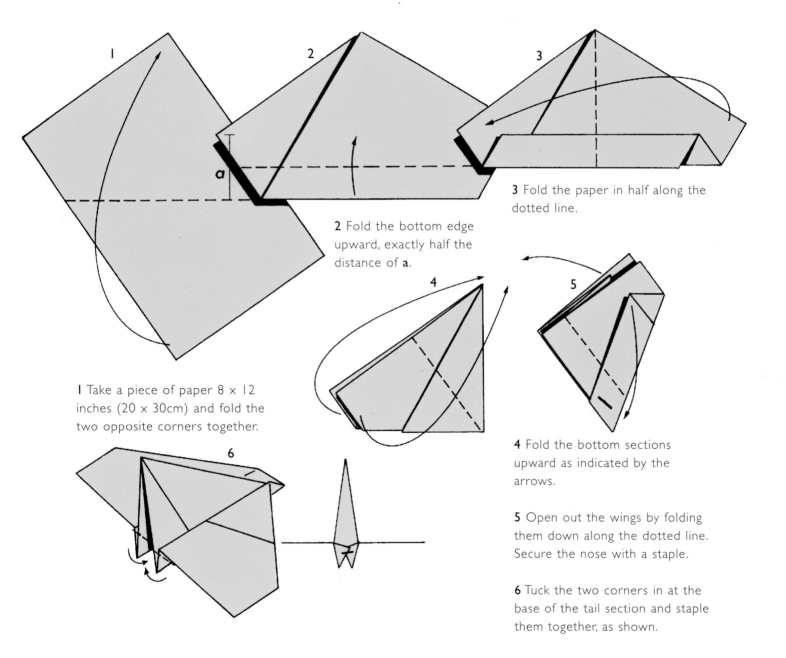

2 Fold the bottom edge upward, exactly half the distance of **a**.

3 Fold the paper in half along the dotted line.

1 Take a piece of paper 8 x 12 inches (20 x 30cm) and fold the two opposite corners together.

4 Fold the bottom sections upward as indicated by the arrows.

5 Open out the wings by folding them down along the dotted line. Secure the nose with a staple.

6 Tuck the two corners in at the base of the tail section and staple them together, as shown.

If a car manufacturer can name its product after the magnificent manta ray, there's no reason why we shouldn't follow suit with this Manta.

By and large, the paper airplane bears a far greater resemblance to the fish than the car does. The front, in particular, has a similar menacing shape. Certain characteristics of the airplane are also similar: great endurance and stability. The Manta is primarily a glider and not well suited to aerobatics.

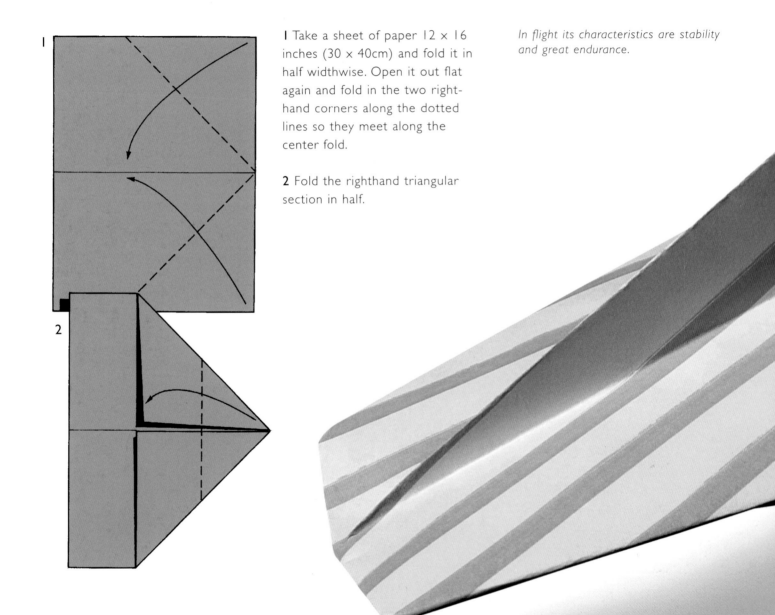

1 Take a sheet of paper 12 × 16 inches (30 × 40cm) and fold it in half widthwise. Open it out flat again and fold in the two right-hand corners along the dotted lines so they meet along the center fold.

2 Fold the righthand triangular section in half.

In flight its characteristics are stability and great endurance.

3 Now fold the two sides inward to meet at the center fold.

4 Turn over and fold in half along the dotted line.

5 Everything has been very easy up to this point; now it gets a little harder. Following the diagram carefully, push the middle section of the tailpiece up through the center by means of an inverted fold. Make wings by folding upward along the dotted lines, one wing to either side.

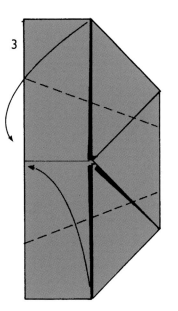

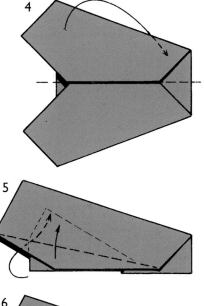

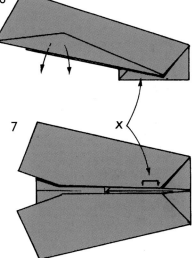

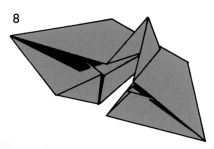

8 To check that all is correct, here is a rear view of the Manta.

6 & 7 Hold the model firmly at point **x** and spread the wings flat. Fold the outside edges of the wings under, joining under the fuselage; staple them together at point **x**. This is a bit tricky and must be done carefully so as not to tear the nose. The staple on the underside not only holds the model in position, but keeps the weight more evenly balanced.

The first plane in the world that could really fly was built by the Wright brothers, Orville and Wilbur. The design of our model recalls it with the small wing in front and larger one behind. Since the Wright brothers' airplane was actually a biplane, you may want to build another wing on top so your model bears an even greater resemblance to the original.

To demonstrate the flying characteristics of this plane to the greatest advantage, it should be allowed to glide freely away from the hand. The small wings should always be in front; this may seem unusual but the early planes were built in this way and the construction of supersonic planes has seen a revival of this type of design. The front edges of the larger wings are curved so that the plane soars farther through the air.

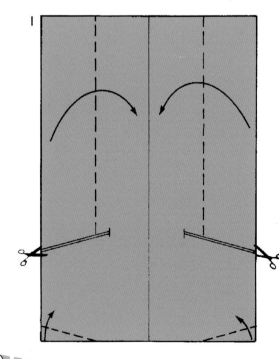

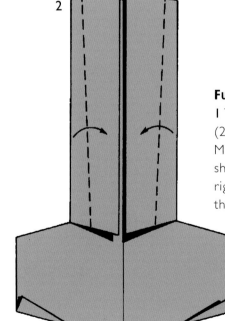

FUSELAGE

I Take a piece of paper 8 x 12 inches (20 x 30cm) and fold it lengthwise. Make a short cut on both sides, as shown. Fold both the lefthand and righthand flaps to the center along the dotted lines, and also fold over the bottom corners along the dotted lines.

2 Fold both sides inward again, along the dotted lines.

The first planes were built like this and the construction of supersonic planes has seen a revival of this design.

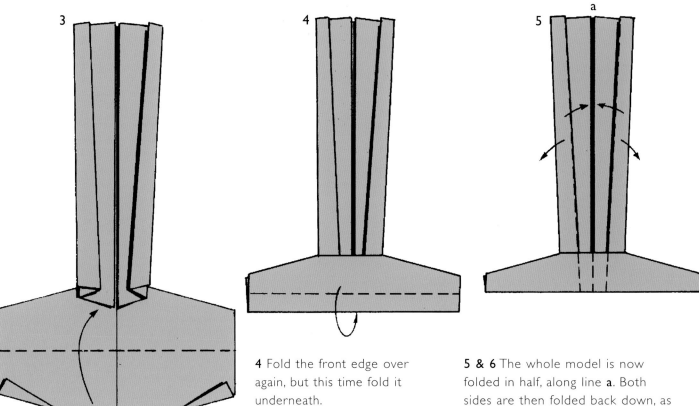

3 Fold up the bottom edge, as illustrated.

4 Fold the front edge over again, but this time fold it underneath.

5 & 6 The whole model is now folded in half, along line **a**. Both sides are then folded back down, as shown in Fig. 6, and the fuselage is completed.

The completed fuselage.

2 Fold the paper in half length-wise. At the same time, press in at the corners of the diagonal folds. If you have done it correctly, the wing shape will be evident.

3 Bend the lefthand edge, that is the front edge of the wings, downward and make a small cut in the center of the back edge as shown. Fold the four loose flaps inside along the dotted lines.

WINGS

1 Take a sheet of paper 8 x 12 inches (20 x 30cm) and fold it in half first lengthwise and then widthwise. Flatten it out and fold it again along the diagonals as illustrated. (It's best to crease backward and forward along each fold a few times.)

4 Bend up the uppermost layer of both wing tips so that they stand vertical to the wings and act as stabilizers. Glue the front edges of the wings together.

5 Join the two sections of the flyer together by fitting the wings over the fuselage as shown and gluing it in place. It is now ready to take to the air. Soon you'll see how well it flies, and that the inventor's theories were well-founded.

Send your Valentine a special way. This one is an alternative to the usual card-in-envelope. It's a fast-flying aircraft which, when accurately trimmed, can perform stunts. The Valentine is also an excellent basic design to use whenever you are in a mood to fashion some interesting, original creations.

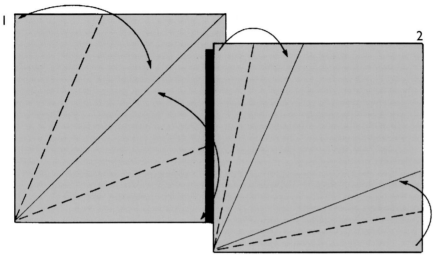

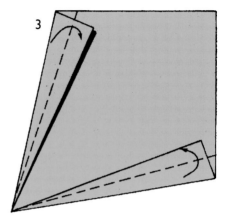

1 Make two diagonal folds in a piece of paper 12 x 12 inches (30 x 30cm) along the dotted lines so that the two edges meet along the center diagonal line. Open flat.

2 Fold each of the two triangles in half along the dotted line.

3 Fold each of the outside triangles in half again along the dotted line.

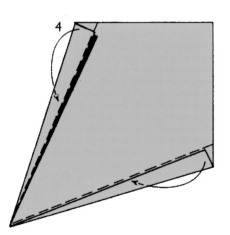

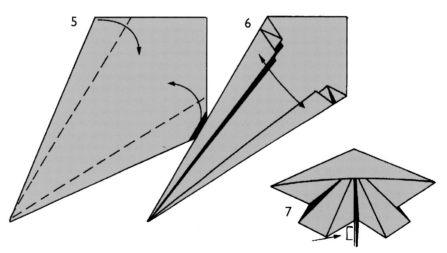

4 Fold each side backward along the dotted line.

5 Now fold the two sides forward again.

6 You now have a series of accordion folds. Unfold them gently to produce the rocket shape.

7 Staple the two innermost folds together, as shown in rear view above, and the Valentine is ready to fly. With the point of the tail you can determine the flight path—the "trim" as they say in flying jargon.

*An original way to speed letters of
love to someone special.*

THE PERFECT PAPER PLANE

It's likely that this is that celebrated and infamous
"paper plane" that school friends could always make more
successfully than you could. Not even offering your
best comics would tempt them to disclose its secret.
Now—better late than never—you can have your revenge.
This Paper Plane is the archetypal model plane.
Once you become totally familiar with this model, the
rest will seem easy. The wings and tail are formed
separately and, once folded, joined together.

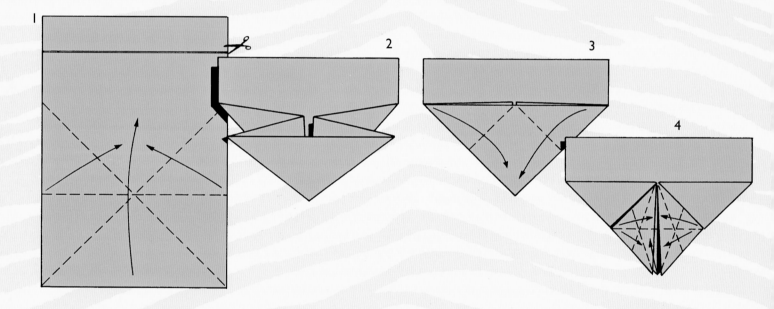

1 Take a piece of paper 8 X 12 inches (20 X 30cm)and cut off one end of the sheet. Put the strip to one side. It will be used later on for the tail. Fold the sheet along the two diagonal lines as shown, then make another widthwise fold through the intersection of the diagonal fold. Make sharp clean creases by folding the paper backward and forward.

2 Fold the lower edge upward while at the same time pressing in at the sides to form an inverted fold. This results in the shape shown.

3 Fold the upper corners of the top layer down to the bottom point along the dotted lines.

4 Now make folds along all the dotted lines as shown in the diagram.

5 At this point, unfold the model as far as shown in the diagram for Step 2. Look at your sheet, and at the illustration at right, at all the creases there now.

Not even a pile of good comics could buy the secret of The Perfect Paper Plane.

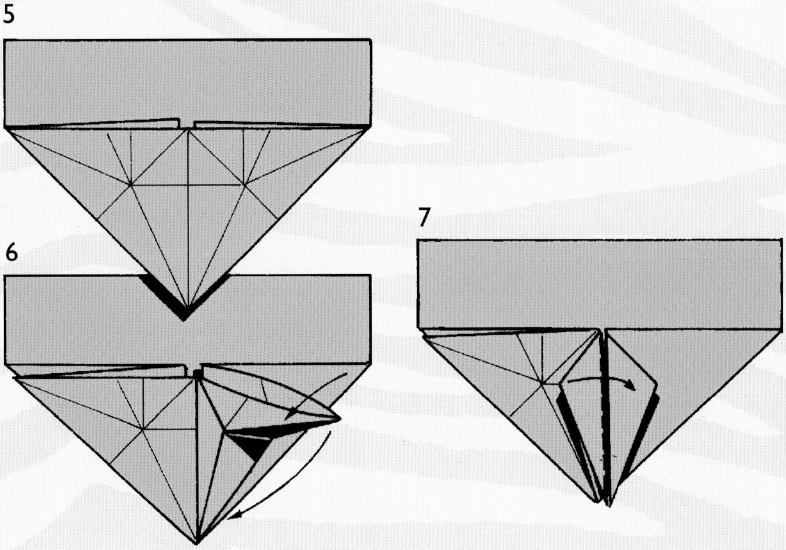

6 This is where things get a bit hairy. Study the diagram before making any moves, and don't give up if it doesn't work the first time. If that so-called school friend could manage it, so can you. Take hold of the right-hand point, pull it toward you, fold it down to the bottom point, and press it down flat.

7 Fold the left side of the figure in the same way you did on on the right-hand side.

5

6

7

8 Now repeat the process in reverse with the left point.

9 From the resulting figure, fold the right side over the left.

10 Bend the back section away from you along the dotted line.

11 Make a center fold, bringing the sides toward you.

12 Arrange the wings in a V shape. Fold the tail piece in half lengthwise and slide it into the wings. The Perfect Paper Plane is now ready for its test flight.

Steps 6 to 9 are the really difficult ones. Once you work on and master those folds, it is clear sailing.

To help clarify, here is a photograph showing the folds from steps 6 to 9.

A latterday Chinese sage said that airplanes without wings wouldn't fly. But what about wings without an airplane? Airplane wings are designed to compensate for the weight of the fuselage, yet it's possible to leave the fuselage out altogether. At least, that's the principle behind Wings. One of the first models in the *Scientific American* International Paper Airplane Competition, it opened up a whole new area of interest. Wings is probably the easiest model to make. Its wing tips may be curved up and down, so the plane makes graceful swoops and spirals, rather like a seagull in a storm. It's important, though, to master the art of launching it.

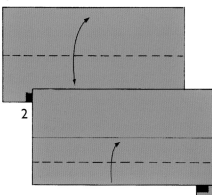

1 Fold a piece of paper 6 × 12 inches (16 × 30cm) in half lengthwise and then open it out again.

2 Fold the lower half up to the middle.

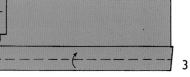

3 Fold this in half again.

4 Stick the edge down with cellophane tape, then cut a slit in the center.

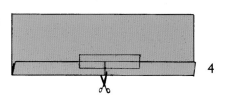

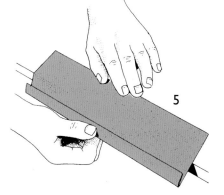

5 Stretch the single layer of paper across the edge of a table to give it a gentle curve.

Wings is now ready for take-off and is launched horizontally from between the forefinger and the thumb. Don't "throw" a paper airplane forward too hard; speed isn't important, and most models perform best if you simply allow them to glide away from your hand. Others require at most a light shove.

The level of difficulty involved in this model isn't high, but it does require some effort. Once the relatively simple steps are completed, the result is beautiful. The Airmail can be made from somewhat thicker paper, enabling it to fly faster and farther. Our Airmail is based on a very fast aircraft design and is a good way to get important notes and messages from one place to another quickly.

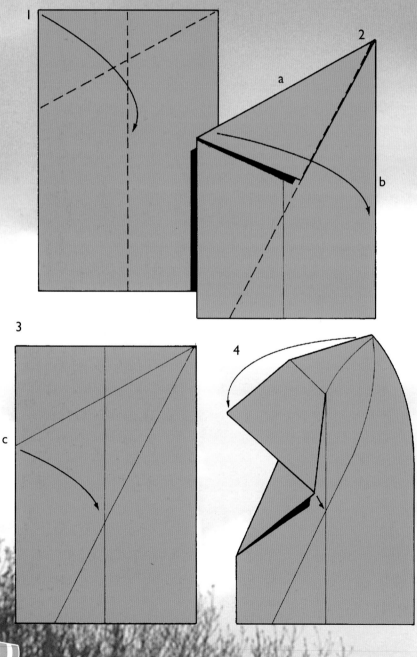

The ultimate way to send airmail, although you can't always be sure where it will land. This one took off in Switzerland by the look of the stamp.

I Take a sheet of paper 8 X 12 inches (20 X 30cm) and fold it in half lengthwise, then open it out flat. Take the top left corner across to the center fold so that the fold also passes through the top right corner.

2 Fold side **a** along side **b** and then open the paper out flat.

3 & 4 Although these steps look complicated, the folds aren't that difficult. Hold the paper at **c** and take that point across to the intersection of the existing creases while, at the same time, taking the top right corner across to the top left corner so they lie flat.

5 This is how your figure should look. Fold the top layer back to the right along the dotted line. Now bring point **d** down toward you. Press flat.

6 Fold the top section in half as shown by the arrow, then fold the whole figure in half lengthwise along the dotted line.

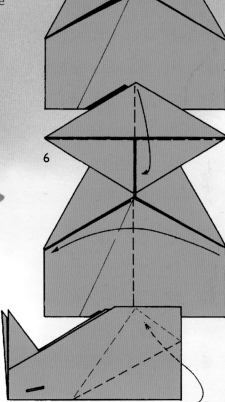

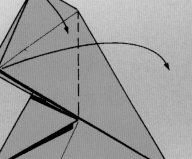

7 Make an inverted fold by pushing the bottom right corner up through the middle of the model to form the tail. Don't make too large a fold or the tail will be out of balance compared to the wing size. Staple the nose together.

8 Unfold the wings along the dotted line, and you have the Airmail. By folding the wing tips up, you can influence the aerodynamics of its flight.

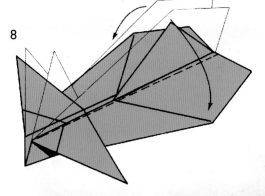

The McDonnell was the creation of aircraft designer
R. Otte, who worked for the American McDonnell Aircraft
Corporation. The first contribution to the *Scientific
American* International Airplane Competition was
produced using McDonnell company stationery.
This airplane was obviously designed by someone with
a particular talent for aeronautical engineering and it
was frequently tested in a wind tunnel.
It's best to use a lighter paper in crafting this model
and to make test flights on a still day.

*The McDonnell, designed by R. Otte and
produced by the McDonnell Aircraft
Corporation.*

1 & 2 Take a sheet of paper 8 × 12 inches (20 × 30cm) and make creases along all the dotted lines. Fold up the bottom edge, tucking in the two sides at the same time, to result in Fig. 2.

3 Fold the two upper points of the triangle down to meet the lower point.

4 Fold along all the dotted lines shown here.

5 Tuck the two points **a** into the "pockets" formed in the lower triangle.

6 Turn the model over. Fold both sides in toward the center, following the dotted lines.

7 Fold the points of these flaps out again, as shown in the diagram. In fact the McDonnell flies very well without this additional detail. Finally make a light crease in the middle of the nose and now it's ready.

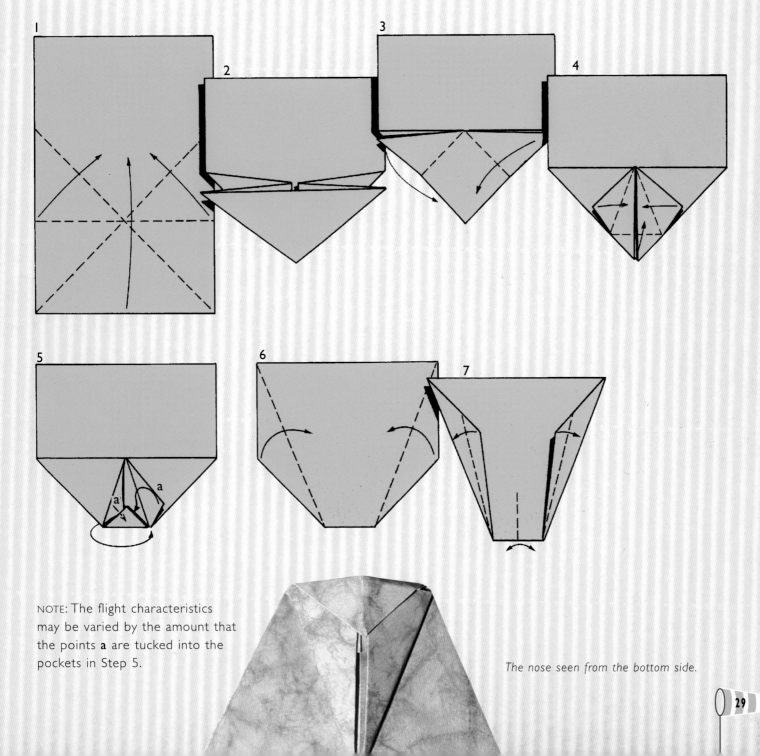

NOTE: The flight characteristics may be varied by the amount that the points **a** are tucked into the pockets in Step 5.

The nose seen from the bottom side.

29

The SX-101 (P)—it sounds mysterious, but many aircraft
are identified in this way. In space exploration,
work is proceeding on projects having such names
as the X-12, LVV-1034, and so on; the letter
and number combinations standing in for
anything without a formal name.
SX-101 (P) sounds like a rocket; the first model
in the SX-100 range (P simply standing for Panther).
Any upcoming variations on the model would likely, and
imaginatively, be called SX-102, SX-103, etc.

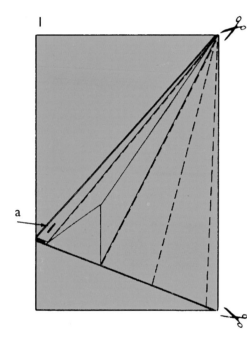

3 Fold the paper in half, tucking in
the sides.

1 Take a piece of paper 8 X 12
inches (20 X 30cm) and cut out the
triangle as directed. Make score
marks along the dotted lines for
easier folding. Fold the two narrow
flaps on either side toward you
along the dotted lines, then make
the two middle folds away from
you. Join them underneath at **a** and
the fuselage is ready.

2 To make the wings, take a piece
of paper 6 x 10 inches (15 x
25cm) and fold it across
both diagonals then
in half length-
wise at
the intersection of the diagonals.

4 Make a short cut in the tip and
bend both the top edges over following the dotted lines. Attach the
front of the wings to the flat back of
the fuselage as seen in the photograph. SX-101 (P) is now ready. It is
one of the simplest models to launch
but, being a rocket, it will need plenty
of propulsion.

The SX-101 (Panther) in its element.

PTERODACTYL (PTERANODON)

The final model in this section on Fantasy Flyers comes from primeval times. It is called the Pterodactyl, due to its similarity to that prehistoric flying reptile. These beasts were not to be trifled with: they seized anything that moved.
The paper reconstruction is, however, more amiable. A faster projectile than even an airplane, it is not very complicated to make. For the best results, make your Pterodactyl out of very light paper because all of its weight is in the nose.

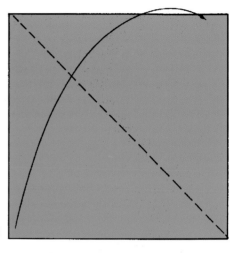

1 Fold a piece of paper 8 x 8 inches (20 x 20cm) in half diagonally.

2 Fold back the top corner so that it lines up exactly with the left edge.

3 Turn over and fold the whole figure in half.

4 Simultaneously press point **x** down and pull point **y** down and over to the right so that the folds are along the dotted lines.

5 Open out the model by folding the upper half back along the dotted line.

The final model in this section on Fantasy Flyers is descended from prehistoric times.

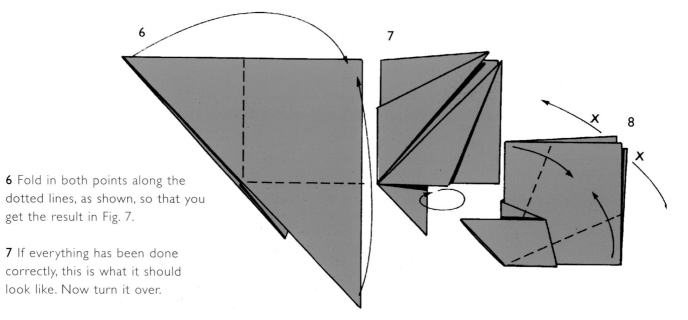

6 Fold in both points along the dotted lines, as shown, so that you get the result in Fig. 7.

7 If everything has been done correctly, this is what it should look like. Now turn it over.

8 Fold the edges in to the center fold as shown by the dotted lines and, at the same time, fold the two points **x** lying underneath out to either side.

Starting from Step 7, the object is turned over and unfolded. The nose is flattened, as shown in 9 and 10.

Pterodactyl construction between Steps 11 and 12 seen from underneath.

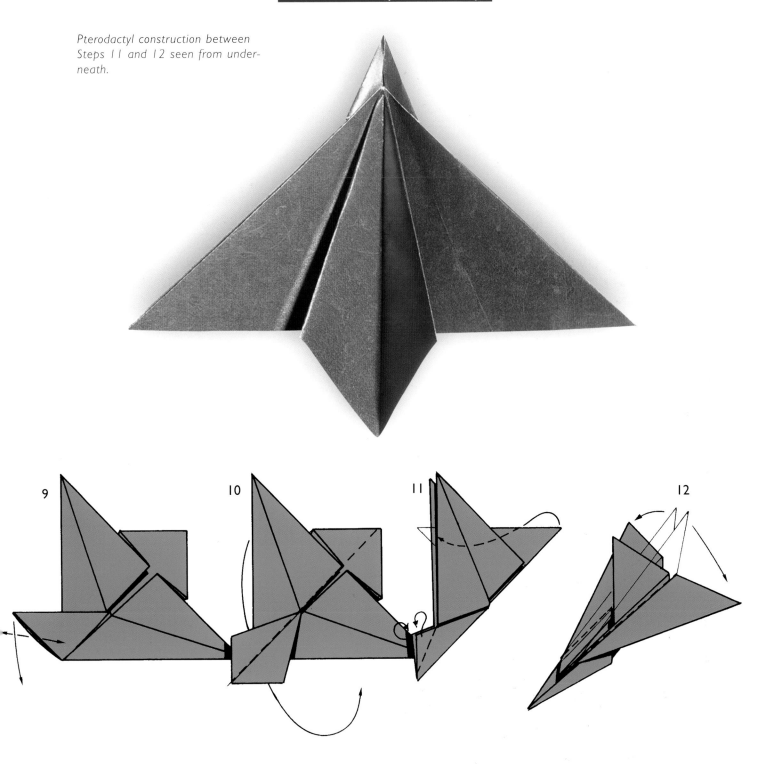

9 Open out the upright triangle and fold it down flat as shown by the arrows.

10 Now, fold the whole thing in half away from you.

11 Tuck in the two points on the nose as shown, following the arrows, then push the tail up and in, using an inverted fold.

12 The only thing left to do is to unfurl the wings along the dotted lines, and the Pterodactyl will be reborn after millions of years.

GENUINE REPRODUCTIONS

Ever since the Wright brothers became the first of our species to fly, a great number of airplanes have been produced—not all of which have performed exactly as planned. In the early days, if they did take off (in many cases they never left the ground), they would plunge suicidally back down to earth. Many great "creations" were smashed beyond repair all too soon, leaving the bewildered pilot totally disillusioned.

These were the teething problems of a new technological era, the memory of which has been captured in silent movies and newer reproductions. During the First World War, the unquestionable value of the airplane was established. Since then, most airplanes have been able to fly quite efficiently; although one does ask oneself just how a jumbo jet manages to remain in the sky, and remark on the Starfighter's resemblance to a tumbling autumn leaf.

But enough; today mankind is well in control of the sky. When Charles Lindbergh became the first to fly across the Atlantic Ocean in the *Spirit of St. Louis*, thousands came to greet him and Parisians became victims of mass hysteria. Today, we board Concorde without a second thought, eager to cover the same distance at supersonic speed. Flying has become nearly as commonplace as train travel.

Nevertheless, many people have at one time dreamed of piloting a jet or flying a fighter plane. In this section, such dreams can to some extent come true, as these paper models reflect the real thing. Each of the five designs here have their own diverse characteristics, both famous and notorious. The French Mirage, the British Tiger Moth, the Swedish Saab 37 Viggen, the Russian

Tupolev Bear and the American F-16 comprise a distinguished international gathering. Just a small comment on the F-16, since airplane enthusiasts will be quick to notice: The stabilizers of our paper F-16 deviate somewhat from the original design. This need not detract from the general impression; after all, such details as proper landing gear or a rotating propeller are not generally included. A folded paper craft is often difficult enough to make. Trying to add such complicated details will only result in a model flying a very short distance—from the table to the wastebasket. Happily, paper is in plentiful supply and perseverance is nearly always rewarded.

The Mirage, made by the French aviation company
Dassault, has proved itself to be one of the best jet
aircraft ever produced. The delta-wing design, which
many aircraft engineers had long forgotten,
was used and gives the Mirage its characteristic shape.
Like the Swedish Saab 37 Viggen, the Mirage is easily
recognizable in flight, even to the uninitiated—
so long as it isn't too high up.
The paper model of the Mirage bears many of
the same characteristics as the original: it regularly
takes part in speed and aerobatic contests and is easily
recognized by its delta wings. One difference,
of course, is the price.

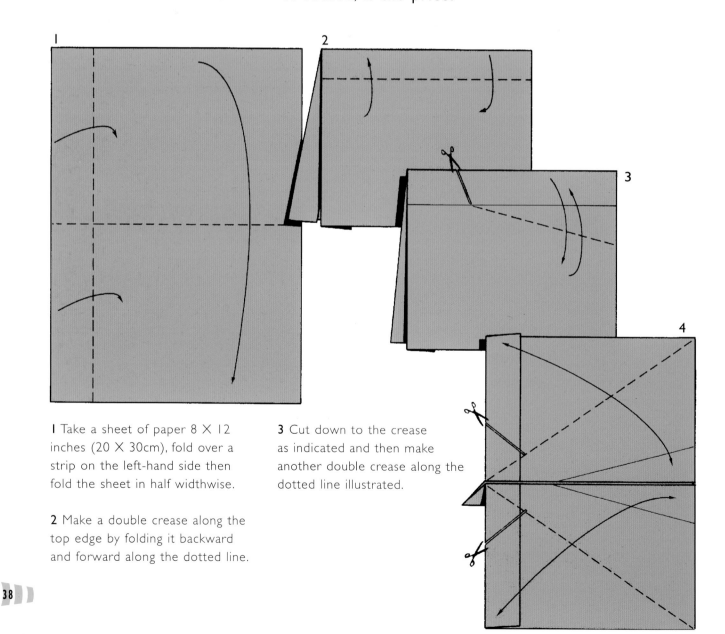

1 Take a sheet of paper 8 X 12
inches (20 X 30cm), fold over a
strip on the left-hand side then
fold the sheet in half widthwise.

2 Make a double crease along the
top edge by folding it backward
and forward along the dotted line.

3 Cut down to the crease
as indicated and then make
another double crease along the
dotted line illustrated.

4 Open out the figure, except for the center section which remains doubled. Make a crease along the diagonal dotted lines and make two cuts from the left-hand edge just beyond the double layer, as shown in the diagram.

The paper model tries to imitate the real thing: the French Mirage in full flight.

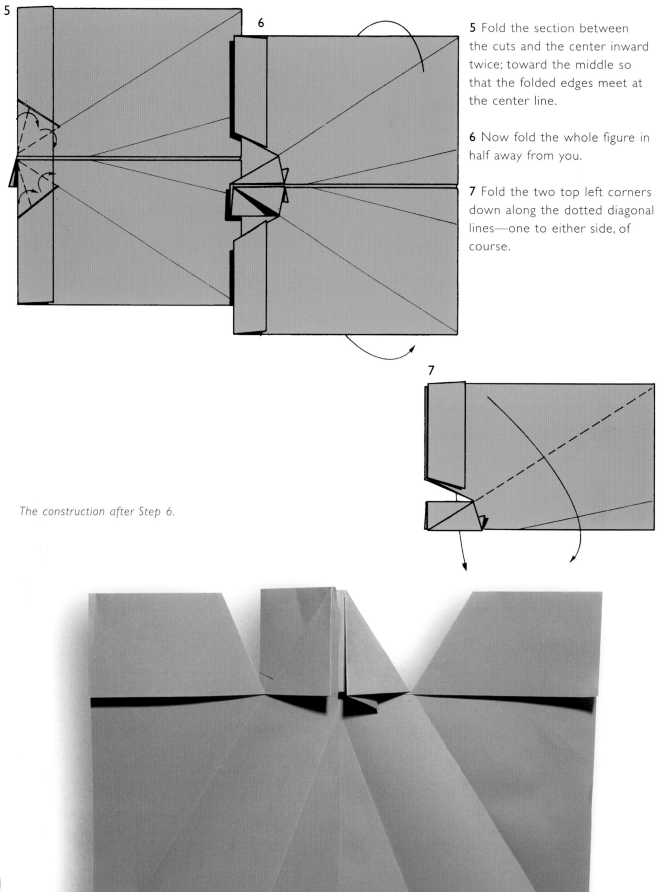

5 Fold the section between the cuts and the center inward twice; toward the middle so that the folded edges meet at the center line.

6 Now fold the whole figure in half away from you.

7 Fold the two top left corners down along the dotted diagonal lines—one to either side, of course.

The construction after Step 6.

The model looks like this after all the Steps up to 9.

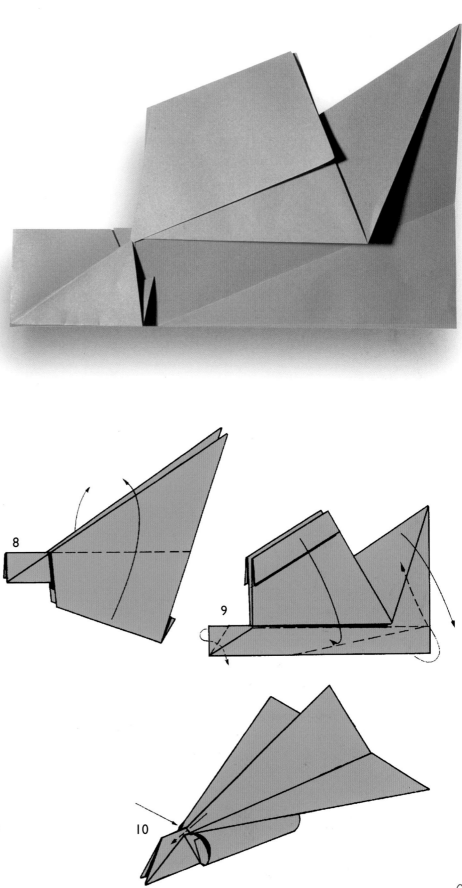

8 Turn up the flaps, which are to become air intakes, by making folds following the line of the fuselage.

9 Make an inverted fold to tuck the nose in, then staple it down. Make an inverted fold in the tail. You can now see how important that cut was in Fig. 3. If you have done it correctly, you can now simply slip the front corner of the tail section into the slit in the fuselage; and the whole thing takes shape (see Fig. 10).

10 Form the air intakes for the jet engines by attaching both folded edges to the side of the fuselage, with the inside edge lying flat against the fuselage. You will find it helpful to curl the paper around your finger to form the right shape. This modification is necessary for good aerodynamics. Finally, if you fold the wings down carefully over the fuselage and air intakes, you will see a genuine replica of the Mirage. Later on you can put flaps in the wings, and the next step after that is the rudder on the tail. Your Mirage should then be able to fly in various directions and in time you and your friends could organize formation flights.

Although this plane is still in existence and often seen in flying demonstrations, it was designed long before the Second World War. Sir Francis Chichester, the celebrated round-the-world yachtsman, made this airplane famous when he flew one to Australia, way back in the nineteen twenties. For years after, it was a popular airplane for training pilots. It's this most famous biplane of all time, the Tiger Moth, on which we modelled our paper airplane reproduction. Contemporaries from the First World War were the legendary Sopwith Camel and the Spad; many of you will likely have read the thrilling tales of the Red Baron and Biggles. Today, the biplane, compared to other designs, is one of the slowest aircraft, yet it has an unbeatable record of aerobatic feats. It is therefore used for stunt flying, and its slow air speed of 36mph (60kph) makes it especially useful for spraying crops.

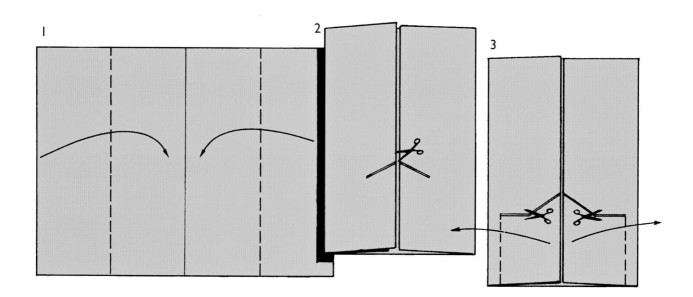

FUSELAGE

1 The initial steps seem easy but be warned: this model is classed as *extremely difficult.* Take a sheet of paper 12 x 16 inches (30 x 40cm) and make a crease down the center. Fold both sides in half to meet along this center crease.

2 Make two short cuts through both the top and bottom layers, as shown in the diagram. A quick look at Fig. 3 would be helpful before making the cuts.

3 Make two more cuts, as indicated, in the top layer only. Fold the two flaps back.

The Tiger Moth: graceful loops ,
simple rolls and, when something
goes wrong, a nosedive .

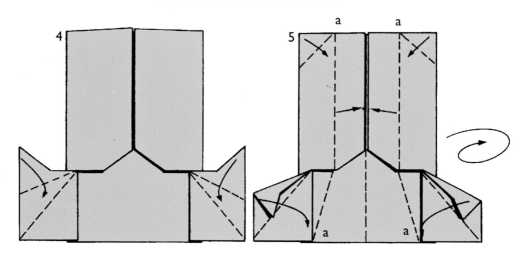

4 Make a diagonal crease in each flap. Fold the top corners down to meet this diagonal line.

5 Fold these two edges inward once again, along the dotted diagonal crease. Up until now it has been fairly easy, but keep close to the wastepaper basket because now things are going to get tough. Make folds going away from you along lines **a**, which you will see slants away at the bottom (Note: The **a** lines are not in the middle of each side section, but closer to the center of the form.) Make a fold along this center line toward you, so all the **a** lines of the fuselage meet along the centerfold. The tip that becomes the nose must be folded inward. Turn the model over.

6 This is how the model should look if everything has been folded according to the instructions. The base of the tail slots into the slit in the fuselage.

7 Using an inverted fold, tuck in the nose. Fold the two top parts outward, along the dotted line, following the line of the fuselage.

Folding the wings is very complicated. It took us three attempts. Do not use thick paper.

WINGS

1 Take a sheet of paper 12 × 16 inches (30 × 40cm) and fold it in half, first widthwise and then lengthwise.

2 Fold the top layer of the bottom lefthand corner along the dotted line, doing the same with the opposite layer. Unfold the paper.

3 Lift the two outside ends of the center line on the long side until they meet, then press the figure flat as shown in Fig. 4.

4 & 5 Fold the point over along the dotted line.

This is how the fuselage should look.

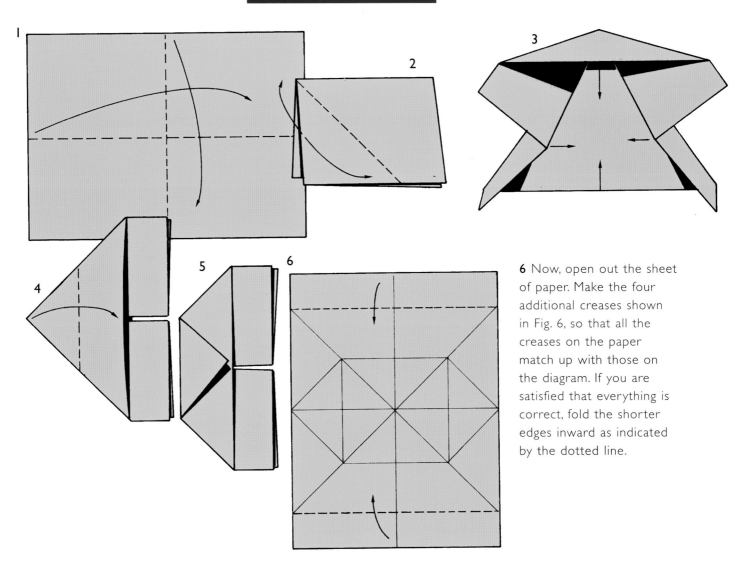

6 Now, open out the sheet of paper. Make the four additional creases shown in Fig. 6, so that all the creases on the paper match up with those on the diagram. If you are satisfied that everything is correct, fold the shorter edges inward as indicated by the dotted line.

The wings after Step 5.

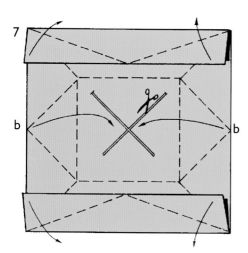

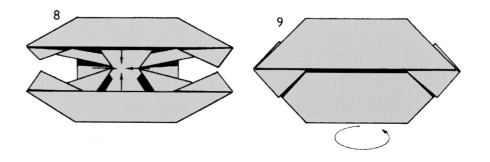

7 Now fold the four corners of these flaps outward and make cuts in the places indicated. It's important that a balance exists between the length and size of the model. Push the **b** points together and press the whole figure down flat so that the four corners of the model lie on top of each another.

8 Actually, it looks harder than it really is. This diagram should help to clarify things.

9 When pressed flat, your model should look like this. Now turn it over.

10 Lift the two points indicated by the arrows toward the center. Follow the fold along the dotted line and press flat.

11 This diagram should make the preceding steps clearer.

Two difficult stages in folding the wings. You may think that you need four hands, but keep trying and you will succeed.

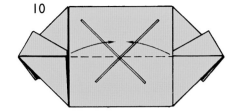

10

11

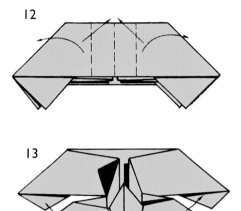

12

13

14

12 Make a fold toward you along the center dotted line and a fold away from you along the dotted lines on either side.

13 It should look like this.

14 Finally, push the fuselage through the hole in the wings and attach them together. The Tiger Moth is ready to make a flight. Soon your model will be doing aerobatics and stunt flying ...after you have made your first ten.

Before take-off: the grand moment of gluing fuselage and wings together.

The pride of the Swedes is the Saab 37 Viggen, a delta-wing jet which, despite some criticism of the wing structure, is still regarded as one of the most advanced fighter planes. The smaller, higher-mounted wings in front of the main wings add to stability at low speeds. The Viggen plays an important role in Sweden's defense plans.

The paper Viggen is a good example of the models of existing designs. It closely resembles the Viggen but, on close inspection, plane enthusiasts will notice some variations. For example, the air inlets on the real Viggen run through to the front wings and the fuselage is proportionately higher behind the tail. In our model, there is no undercarriage, no jet engine, and no weapons; nonetheless our Viggen flies beautifully.

The pride of the Swedes in a paper
model: the Saab 37 Viggen, a unique
aircraft.

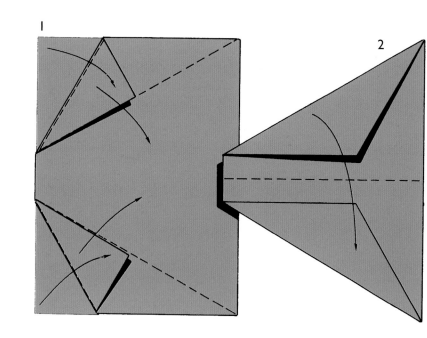

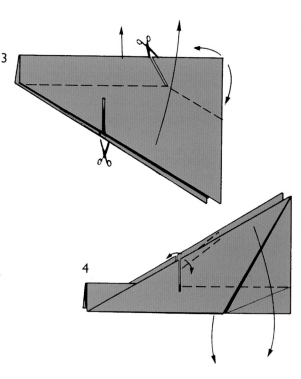

1 Take a piece of paper 12 x 16 inches (30 x 40cm) and fold the two left-hand corners over to the dotted lines as shown. Then fold again along the dotted lines.

2 Fold the complete model in half as shown, with the flaps inside.

3 Make cuts in the paper as indicated and crease the tail by folding it backward and forward over the diagonal dotted line. Fold the wings up on both sides along the straight dotted line.

4 Fold the front edges of the large delta wings down along the dotted lines at the cuts, then fold the wings down on both sides along the straight dotted line, as shown in the diagram.

5 Make an inverted fold in the tip of the nose and push the base of the tail through the slit. Fold the wings up along the dotted line and the tips of the delta wings under as shown.

6 Secure the nose with a paper-clip or staple. Push the base of the delta wings up slightly to form air inlets for the jet engine, and then staple or glue in place (see arrow). Fold the small front wings along the dotted line.

7 If your Saab 37 Viggen looks exactly like this illustration, it's ready for take-off.

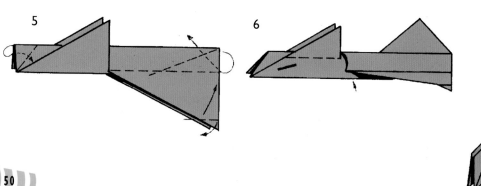

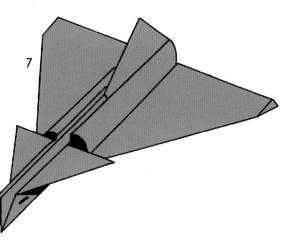

The Russian Tupolev is a unique airplane in aircraft history. The "Bear," as it is commonly called in the West, is one of the largest aircraft in the world and was believed—wrongly—to be a jet. It has huge V-form wings and four turbo-jets that power immense propellers which move the craft through the sky. Aviation experts have said that the plane's design should inhibit it from flying, but the Tupolev proves the opposite. Reports say the gigantic propellers explode against one another due to the aircraft's vibrations.

If necessary, this enormous plane can remain in the sky for twenty-four hours. The same goes for its little brother, our model, speaking relatively that is. The length of air time must be somewhat proportional; a flight lasting twenty-four seconds is, however, not impossible. This Bear is also a wonderful glider. The turbines and propellers have obviously been omitted.

The Tupolev (Bear) is an excellent glider.

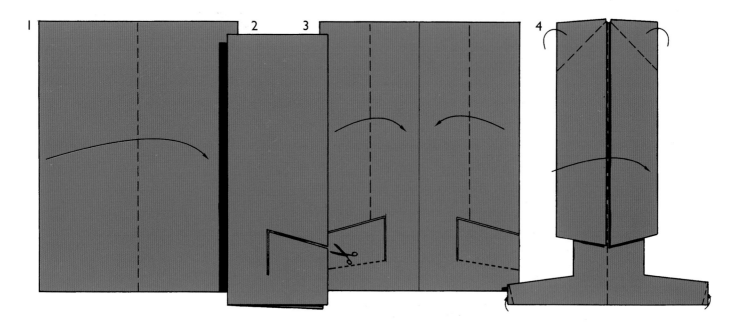

FUSELAGE

1 Take a sheet of paper 12 x 16 inches (30 x 40cm) and fold it in half.

2 Make a cut through both la yers of paper as indicated.

3 Open the paper out flat and fold both sides inward to the center along the dotted lines.

4 Fold back the top cor ners to make the nose. Fold the loose flaps of the tail section under and also fold under the tips of the tail as indicated. Now fold the whole model in half.

5 Fold the top edge of the whole fuselage to either side , as shown.

6 Once again, make folds along the whole length of the fuselage to either side .

WINGS AND TAIL

1 Take a sheet of paper 12 x 16 inches (30 x 40cm) and fold it in half.

2 Make creases across both left-hand cor ners by folding them backward and for ward along the dotted lines.

3 Open out the paper, then fold it in half again tucking in the sides.

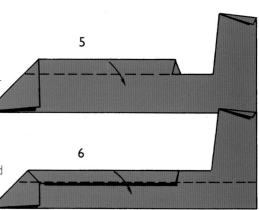

The result once the fuselage is finished.

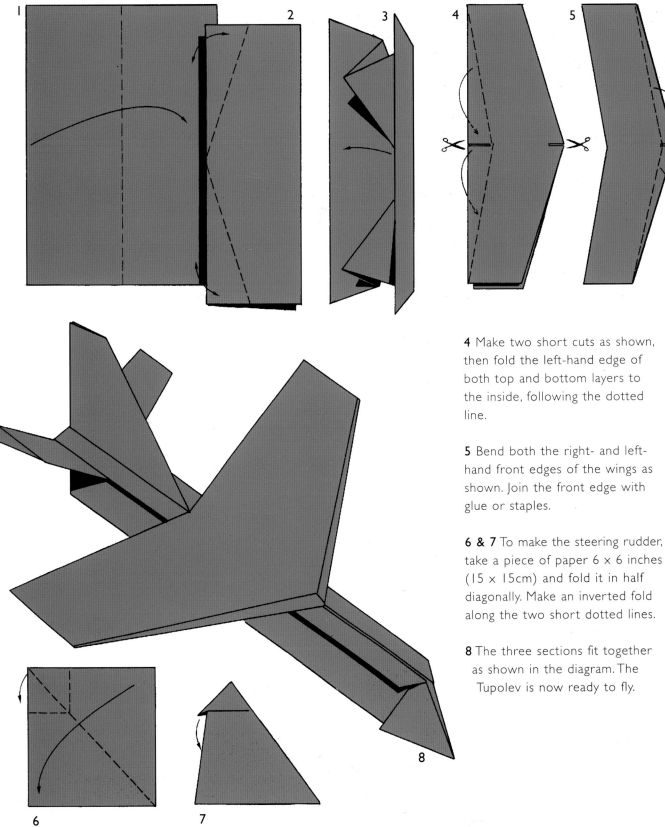

4 Make two short cuts as shown, then fold the left-hand edge of both top and bottom layers to the inside, following the dotted line.

5 Bend both the right- and left-hand front edges of the wings as shown. Join the front edge with glue or staples.

6 & 7 To make the steering rudder, take a piece of paper 6 x 6 inches (15 x 15cm) and fold it in half diagonally. Make an inverted fold along the two short dotted lines.

8 The three sections fit together as shown in the diagram. The Tupolev is now ready to fly.

The F-16 Fighting Falcon, manufactured by General Dynamics, has become a controversial aircraft during its brief history. It is a jet with extraordinary potential and the most up-to-date equipment. Computers perform an important role; it's been said that it's not the pilot who flies the F-16, but the F-16 that flies the pilot.

Our paper F-16 was modelled on a design by Eiji Nakamura, a well-known Japanese expert on folded paper planes, and its shape is perhaps the most pleasing of the whole series. Apart from that, the F-16 is a very good model that flies quickly and can perform aerobatics. You can try using different types of paper when making it, but don't use anything too light.

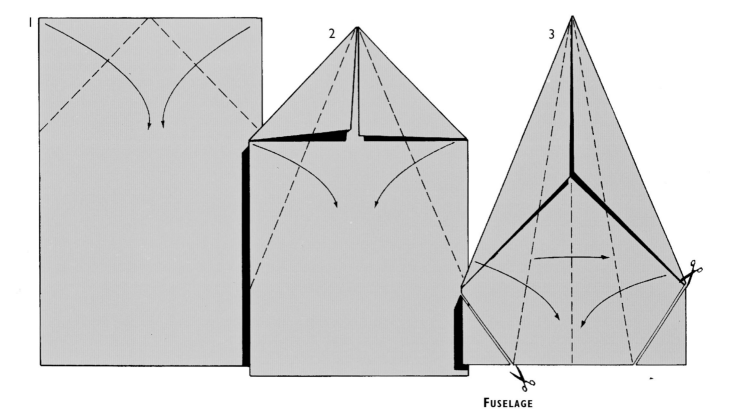

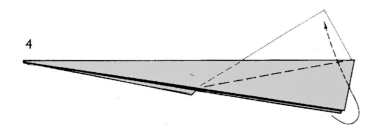

FUSELAGE

1 Take a sheet of paper 12 x 16 inches (30 x 40cm) and fold the top corners inward along the dotted lines.

2 Fold inward again along the dotted lines, so that all the folds meet at the top center point.

3 Fold the outside edges inward along the dotted lines for the third time and then cut off the corners as directed. Fold the whole model in half away from you along the center line.

4 Fold the tail section backward and forward along the dotted line, and push up the center using an inverted fold.

The paper F-16 was modelled on a design by Eiji Nakamura, a well-known Japanese expert on folded paper planes.

An original present: The F-16 folded from bank notes. This model is made of Euro bank notes. The wing tips are folded upwards. The tail wings stay straight.

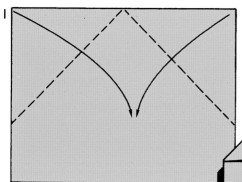

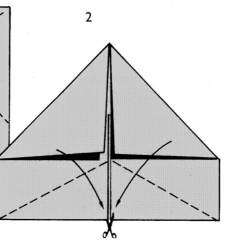

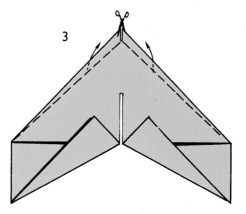

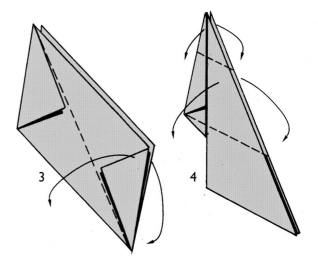

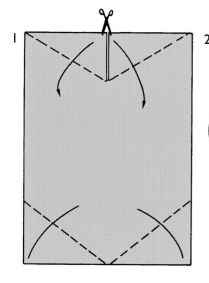

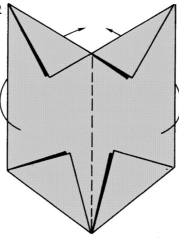

WINGS

1 Take a sheet of paper 8 X 12 inches (20 X 30cm) and fold in the two top corners of the long side so they meet in the middle.

2 Make a cut as shown and fold the resulting flaps upwards along the dotted lines.

3 Make a small cut in the top point, and bend the edges toward you along the dotted lines. This view is of the underside of the wings.

TAIL

1 Make a short cut along the center line of a paper 8 X 12 inches (20 X 30cm) and fold the corners along the dotted lines. Now fold the lower corners upwards as shown.

2 Fold the model in half away from you along the dotted line.

3 Fold the flaps to either side along the diagonal dotted line.

4 Fold the tip of the tail open to either side along the dotted line and then fold the tail open along the lower dotted line again to either side. Glue the edges of the bottom half together.

5 Attach the wings to the top side of the fuselage so that the tail end fits into the ready-made groove, and glue the whole thing together. Attach the tail by slotting it over the fuselage. The F16 is now ready for its maiden flight.

COMPETITION CRAFT

There's no sport without competition and flying paper airplanes is now considered to be a sport. America got off to a flying start and originated the rules for the contests. Here are the categories: longest flight (in yards/meters, or if you are lucky, miles/kilometers), longest time in the air, aerobatics, and best loops or most impressive nose dive. Obviously, there could be further competition classes.

Competition has always been an important element in flying; more than just a few half-crazy pilots made valiant efforts to cross the Atlantic in rickety little planes before Charles Lindbergh succeeded in the *Spirit of St. Louis*. The 'round-the-world yachtsman, Sir Francis Chichester, attempted to fly around the world in a Tiger Moth. Amelia Earhart was the first woman to complete a nonstop flight from America to Japan. These are the kinds of feats that model flyers try to emulate on a smaller scale. You could, for instance, find a large pond in a nearby park and try to reach the other side with your best competition craft, or you could organize speed contests.

Competition craft should be very carefully folded. There are eight designs here. Experiment with different types of paper and decide for yourself which is best and, if necessary, make small modifications to improve performance. Care should be taken to ensure there are enough models entered in each class.

Learn the abilities of each model and practice the best way to launch them. The

The Sprinter, a very fast fighter plane.

aerobatics performed by competition craft are similar to those by other models. Numerous stunts can be attempted: a loop, in which the airplane turns a full circle, is obtained by turning the flaps upwards. A roll, in which the plane revolves around its axis, is achieved by folding one flap upward and the other one downward. A corkscrew is a special kind of roll. If the paper airplane also has tail flaps, many more aerobatic maneuvers are possible.

Stunts may be carried out in many different ways and sequences. Naturally, when performing aerobatics there is always the risk of crashing, but you can always make a new paper airplane. For formation flying, use only sturdily built models.

The Cirrus 75 is a long-range specialist.

The name Cirrus 75 wasn't chosen at random. This model
was named after the best and most up-to-date glider
because it has the same qualities as its big brother.
Our Cirrus 75 can also make long-range flights, and it is
especially successful starting from a high point such as a
balcony or upstairs window. This plane is, therefore,
particularly suited for "longest flight" and "longest
lasting flight" competition classes.
It's best to use lightweight paper.

The Cirrus 75 can make long-range flights.

1 & 2 Take a sheet of paper 8 X 12 inches (20 X 30cm), fold it first along the diagonal lines, then make a horizontal fold through the intersection as shown. Tuck in each side while folding up the botton edge; see Fig. 2.

3 Fold the two corners down along the dotted lines.

4 Cut out the sections indicated in the top half (to make the sides symmetrical, fold the model in half before cutting the sections out).

Once this is completed, fold the airplane in half along the center line and then fold the wings back along the dotted lines to either side of the center. Fold the tail tips along the dotted lines. Look closely at the diagrams to better understand the procedure.

5 Fasten or staple the sides of the tail together below the fold. The flaps on the wings can be folded upward or downward so that aerobatics and boomerang stunts are possible.

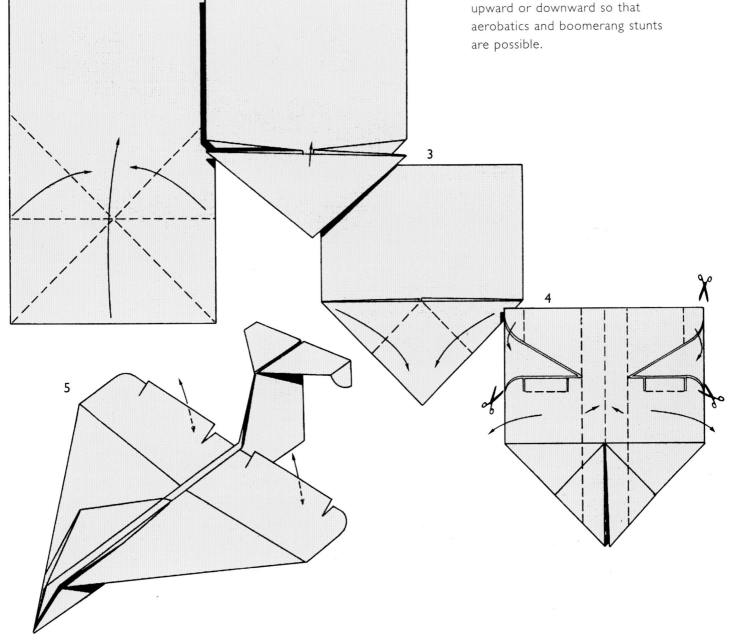

Although when you look at this airplane you will not immediately think of the British Hunter, its flight performance will certainly remind you of that fantastic jet airplane. The delta wings are the dominant feature of this plane. The large tail section guarantees it sufficient stability and the flaps on the wings, based on what is known in aeronautics as the "slotted flap" principle, improve its gliding efficiency. The Hunter is extremely fast and will produce some startling performances for you after only a short training period.

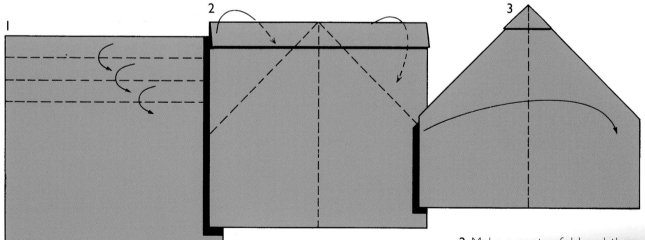

1 Take a piece of paper 10 x 12 inches (25 x 30cm)) and fold the top edge over three times to make a thick edge.

2 Make a center fold and then fold the top corners back along the dotted lines.

3 Fold the whole model in half.

The Hunter is a very fast airplane that will produce startling results for you once you've gotten the hang of it.

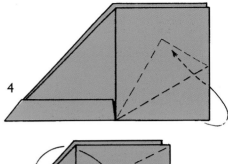

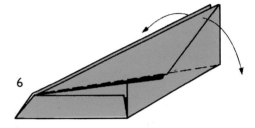

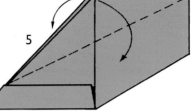

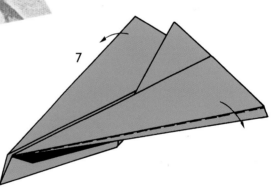

4 Fold the bottom right corner backward and forward along the dotted line, then invert the fold to make the tail.

5 Fold the top edges of the wings along the dotted lines.

6 Fold the wings along the dotted lines once again.

7 Make a tapering fold along the edge of each wing. This improves the airplane's gliding ability; the Hunter is now ready.

SPRINTER (CHEETAH)

The Sprinter is good at just about everything. It is shaped like a supersonic jet and is capable of winning top marks in competitions. It's no slouch in the aerobatic area either, compared to other models, due to the special design of the middle section, where the nose flap is folded and fastened over the wings. This widens the fuselage and improves the airplane's performance. The Sprinter is an all-round model that can go anywhere and be ready to fly at any time.

The Sprinter can do everything and go anywhere.

1 Take a sheet of paper 12 x 14 inches (30 x 35cm) and make a center fold lengthwise. Fold both sides in half so that they meet on the center fold.

2 Fold the corners backward and forward along the dotted lines.

3 Fold the corners over to meet the folds you have just made.

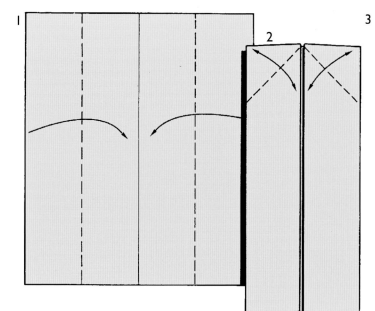

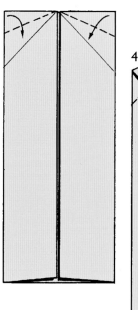

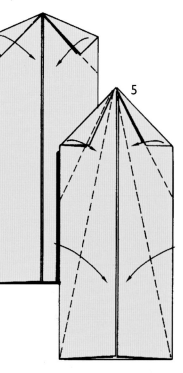

4 Once again, fold the top edges over along the dotted lines.

5 Make creases along the long diagonal dotted lines by folding backward and forward. Fold in the top corners to meet these dotted lines.

6 Fold the whole model in half away from you.

7 Fold the wings up along the existing crease. Now, make an inverted fold in the tail, following the dotted lines and open out the wings.

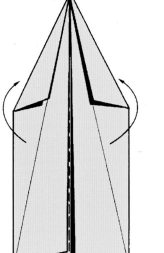

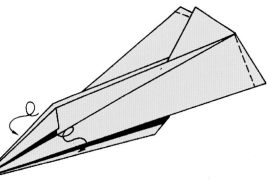

8 Finally, fold the nose section over the wings to either side and glue or staple it to the underside of the fuselage. You'll find that, by easing the outer folds open, the folds fit inside each other neatly. Flaps may be made at the back of the wings, but the form these take really depends on the class you want your Sprinter to fly in.

The Acrobat is specifically designed for one purpose—
aerobatics or stunt-flying. This type of stunt plane is
distinguished by its hard nose, the original wing
shape and the large wing flaps.
Over a distance of 5 to 10 yards, this airplane can perform
a complete loop or roll. Its repertoire also includes a
double somersault with a backward twist. In addition to
being fun to fly, the Acrobat is quick and fairly
simple to make. Its greatest advantage is that it
can beat all the other models at aerobatics.
But watch out—the danger is that it may deviate from
its assigned course and crash into furniture,
the family pet, or even a barbecue!

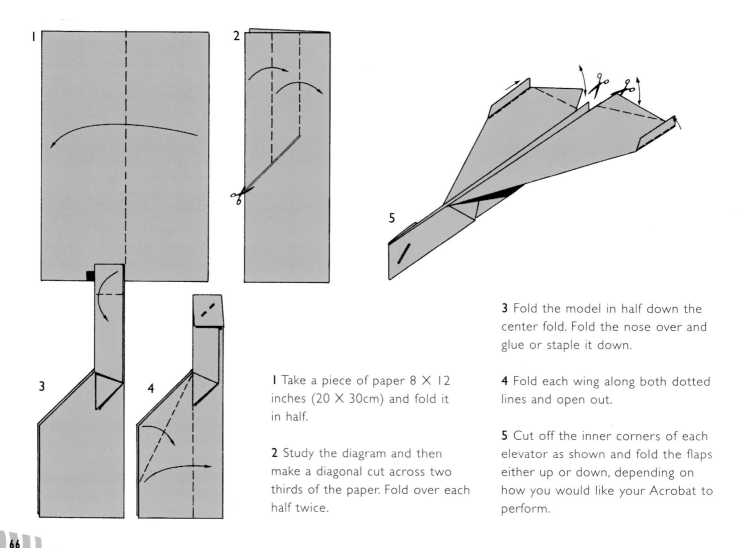

3 Fold the model in half down the
center fold. Fold the nose over and
glue or staple it down.

4 Fold each wing along both dotted
lines and open out.

5 Cut off the inner corners of each
elevator as shown and fold the flaps
either up or down, depending on
how you would like your Acrobat to
perform.

1 Take a piece of paper 8 × 12
inches (20 × 30cm) and fold it
in half.

2 Study the diagram and then
make a diagonal cut across two
thirds of the paper. Fold over each
half twice.

*Over a distance of 5 to 10 yards, this
model can complete a roll or a loop.*

This model is extremely headstrong. Its flight begins like that of a jet but, once in the air, it unfurls its wings and demonstrates its fine gliding abilities, a feature that enables it to cover great distances. The Sailplane is a first-class contender for a prize in the long-distance class. The design is based on sound aerodynamic principles, which account for its fine performance.
Put some weight behind your throw to get it going. You will see how flight occurs in two phases—first the rapid take-off and then a slower glide, during which the wings expand considerably. Experience has shown that using a lightweight paper in its construction will maximize the Sailplane's in-flight time.

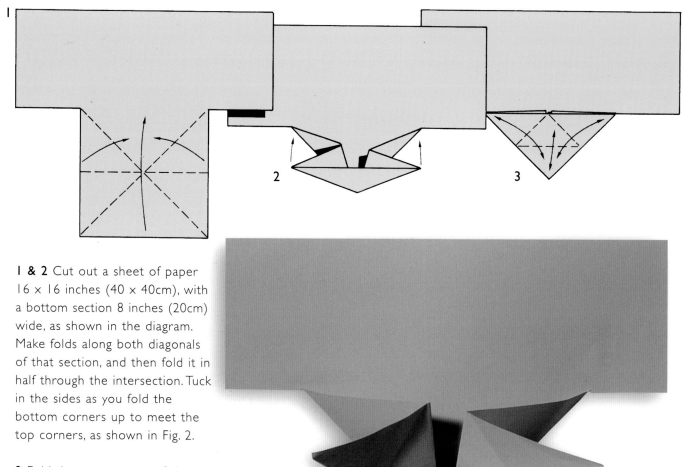

1 & 2 Cut out a sheet of paper 16 x 16 inches (40 x 40cm), with a bottom section 8 inches (20cm) wide, as shown in the diagram. Make folds along both diagonals of that section, and then fold it in half through the intersection. Tuck in the sides as you fold the bottom corners up to meet the top corners, as shown in Fig. 2.

3 Fold the two corners of the top layers and the bottom point backward and forward along the dotted lines.

This is how it should look between Steps 3 and 4.

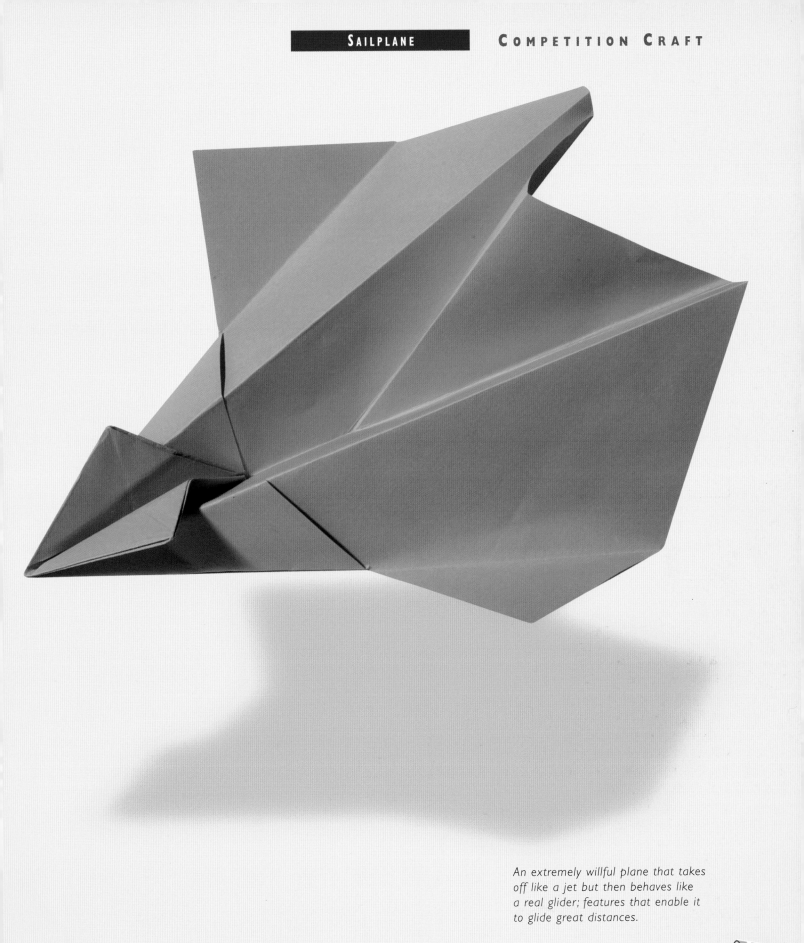

An extremely willful plane that takes off like a jet but then behaves like a real glider; features that enable it to glide great distances.

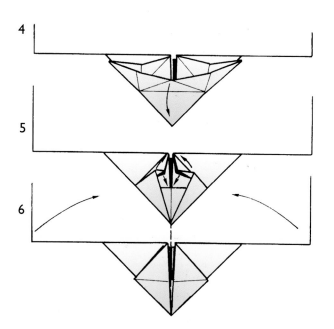

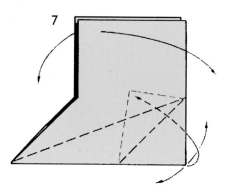

4 & 5 This part is complicated. Push the outside corners of the triangle inside the top layer and downward so that the points lie inside the point at the bottom of the triangle. This is much easier if you have already made good folds in the previous step.

6 As soon as this is successfully completed, fold the whole figure in half along the dotted line.

7 Make a long diagonal fold from the nose, as shown by the dotted line, and then fold the bottom corner backward and forward along the dotted line and push it up in an inverted fold to make the tail. Unfold the wings along the diagonal fold.

8 All that remains now is to fold the wing tips up along the dotted lines.

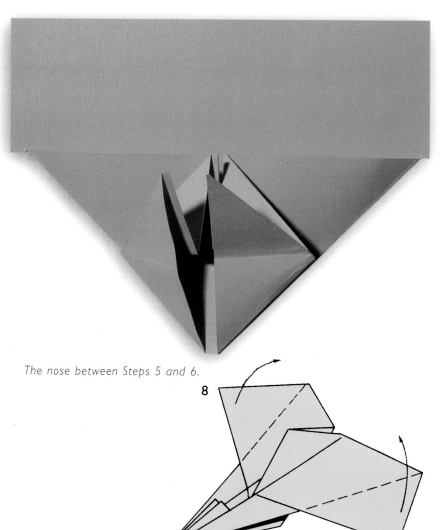

The nose between Steps 5 and 6.

This superb airplane, which won a prize at the *Scientific American* International Airplane Competition, was designed by the Japanese professor and origami expert, James M. Sakoda. This model is a fine example of origami, the Japanese art of paper folding. It is a very fast airplane and excellent for aerobatic stunt-flying. The Sakoda is not hard to fold. At first glance it could be a prototype for a new supersonic airplane—a powerful space-cruiser.

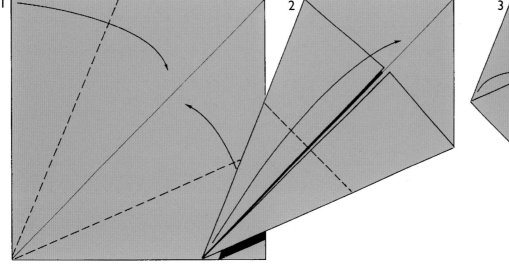

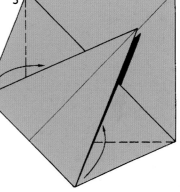

1 Fold two corners of a sheet of paper 12 x 12 inches (30 x 30cm) inward, to meet along a diagonal center line.

2 Fold up the resulting point along the dotted line.

3 Fold the sides underneath the point you have just folded. See Fig. 4.

This is how it should look between Steps 3 and 4.

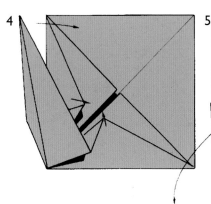

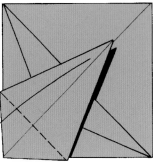

4 This diagram makes it clearer.

5 Fold the point back again along the dotted line and push the model flat.

6 Fold the two edges over to the center line as shown in the diagram and press down flat.

7 Fold the wings away from you along the dotted lines, then fold the whole model in half along the center line.

8 Bend the tips of the wings, as indicated.

A detailed picture of the result after Step 6.

The Sakoda is not difficult to make.

"Elementary, my dear Watson," said Sherlock Holmes
to his perplexed assistant on completing a fine piece of
detective work. The skills of the great detective may
also be applied to designing airplanes. By investigating
particular features of different airplanes, and using your
own powers of deduction to combine the most
complementary ones, you may indeed find the
formula for a whole new design.
The Sherlock Special combines certain features of the
Flying Arrow (pages 88–89) and the Sailplane (pages
68–70) to produce the finest characteristics of both.
Ideas have come from other designs in this book
to solve one puzzle of aeronautical design but,
as in many investigative affairs, there is often
more than one solution.

*The Sherlock Special —an airplane
combining the finest characteristics
of two other models.*

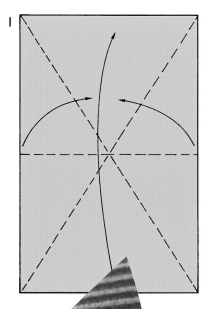

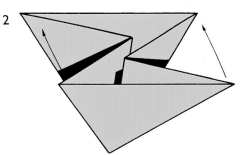

3

WINGS

1 & 2 Fold a sheet of paper 8 X 12 inches (20 X 30cm) along both diagonals and then in half widthwise. Having made good creases, fold the sheet in half while simultaneously tucking in the sides as shown in Fig. 2.

3 Cut a slot through the center of the triangle. Fold up the top layer of both the corner sections as indicated.

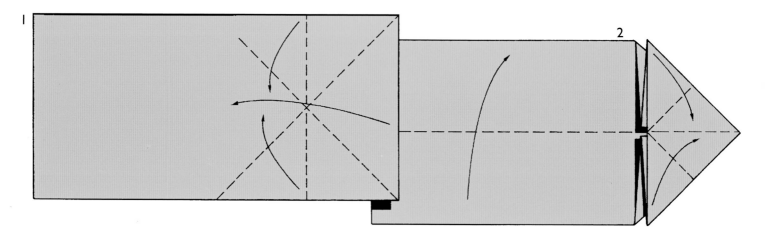

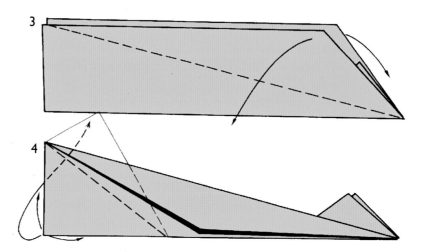

FUSELAGE

1 Fold a sheet of paper 8 x 16 inches (20 x 40 cm) along the dotted lines, as you did with the wings. Also in the same way, fold it in half, tucking in the sides.

2 Fold in the outside points of the resulting triangles along the dotted lines to the center line. Then, fold the whole model in half lengthwise.

3 Fold each side outwards along the dotted lines.

4 Fold backward and forward along the dotted line to make an inverted fold for the tail. Fasten the nose with glue, cellophane tape, or a staple.

5 Slot the wings over the tail-piece and glue the two sections together.

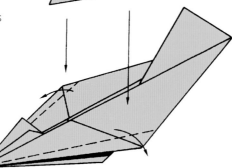

The Sherlock Special is now ready to explore high altitudes. A modification can be made by folding down the sides of the fuselage along the dotted lines. This makes the fuselage more compact and, with this refinement, it will perform loops and rolls with careful adjustment of the various moving parts.

Although Great Britain is not yet using the Euro bank notes, the Sherlock Special looks "special" folded from them.

By joining together several similar sections of a familiar design, an entirely original concept is created—one that has moved a few light years away from conventional paper airplanes. The resulting Flying Dragon is based on the Sherlock Special design but, as you can see clearly from the picture, it takes at least three airplanes to make one dragon.

It takes at least three airplanes to make one Flying Dragon.

NOSE

1 & 2 Take a sheet of paper 8 × 8 inches (20 × 20cm). Make folds along both diagonals and then across the center intersection. Fold it in half, tucking in the sides as the arrows indicate. Turn down the corners of the top layer.

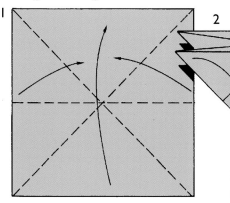

3 Fold in half along the center dotted line and then fold down the wing sections to either side along the dotted lines.

4 This is what the result should look like.

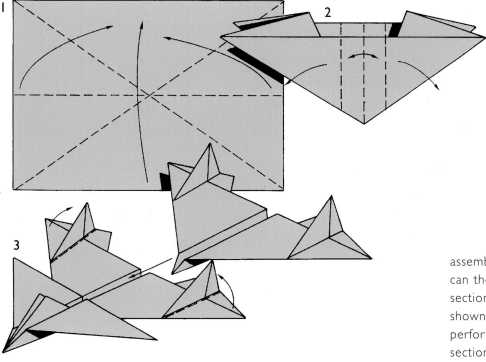

WINGS

1 Take a sheet of paper 8 × 12 inches (20 × 30cm) and make folds along the dotted lines as shown, with a lengthwise fold through the intersection.

2 Fold in half as before, tucking in the edges. Following the diagram, fold the whole model into a V-shape along the dotted lines and turn up the top layer of the wing tips.

3 Insert the wing into the ready-made nose and fuselage section as shown in the diagram, and glue it in tight. This is the first step in assembling the Flying Dragon. You can then add on as many wing sections as you wish—two are shown here. It's best to test flight performance in-between adding sections. We added on five wing sections but had to stop when the waiter in the Chinese restaurant we were in didn't want us to use any more paper table napkins—although he agreed our creation looked like a real dragon. This was after it crash landed in a plate of chop suey five tables away. Heavy air traffic, however, prevailed until closing time.

EXPERIMENTAL MODELS

Man had been experimenting with paper aircraft long
before he conquered the skies. It's therefore logical
to use paper in designing models for the future.
A number of different ones are tested in this section;
it would be interesting to see the performance
of full-size versions.
Futuristic models based on energy-saving principles are
included here: the Catapult Plane (pages 81–85) could
prove useful in the real world, and also the revolutionary
new helicopter design (pages 90–91) might possibly
fill a new niche in the world of flight.

And the future?
Well, don't forget that it took years to develop Concorde
but, after all that, it closely resembles the schoolboy's
traditional paper plane. Why should history not repeat
itself? The four models on the following pages are just
preliminary designs, so feel free to carry out further
experiments or make your own modifications
if you think they will improve the model.
In years to come your ideas may well be quite realistic.

The Flying Fish. See page 86.

The main feature of the Catapult Plane is its great speed.
Its firing mechanism is very efficient and has been used
as a weapon of war throughout the centuries.
This plane is "fired" in the same way as those
classroom (or office!) paper pellets were, with the help
of a rubber band. You might easily get blisters on your
thumbs from a continuing barrage of pellets, but this
design removes that danger and keeps the fun. The
Catapult Plane is a design of the future because
no one today believes this firing technique
would really work—not without using
enormous rubber bands!
It's best to use very thin paper for this model.

*You could get fired up easily, launching
your Catapult Plane.*

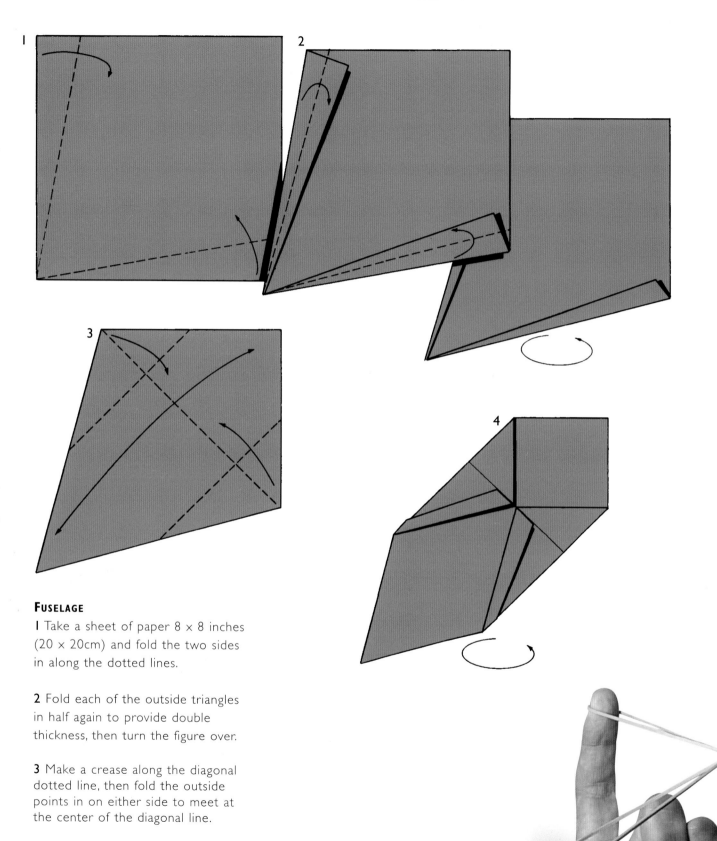

FUSELAGE

1 Take a sheet of paper 8 × 8 inches (20 × 20cm) and fold the two sides in along the dotted lines.

2 Fold each of the outside triangles in half again to provide double thickness, then turn the figure over.

3 Make a crease along the diagonal dotted line, then fold the outside points in on either side to meet at the center of the diagonal line.

4 The figure should look like this; now turn it over once again.

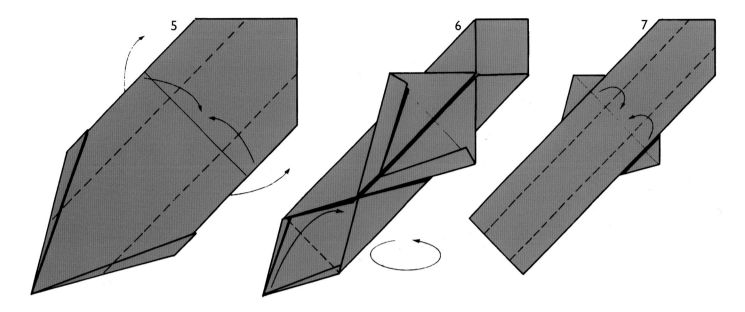

5 Fold both sides in toward the center and, at the same time, open out the underlying flaps.

6 Fold up the nose tip and tuck it in as shown in the diagram, then turn the model over again.

7 Fold along the dotted lines as indicated by the arrows.

With or without a nose "clip," the Catapult Plane is fired with a rubber band.

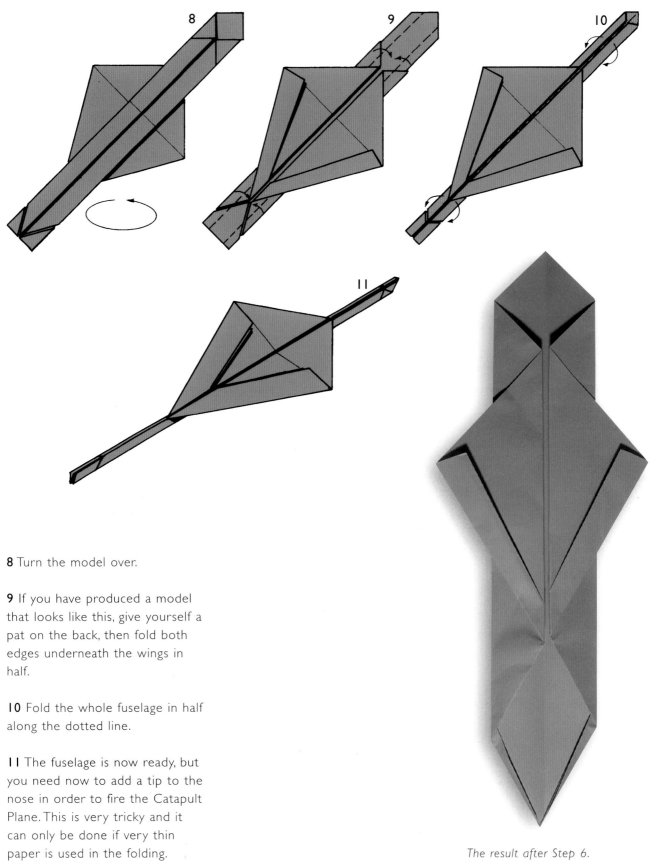

8 Turn the model over.

9 If you have produced a model that looks like this, give yourself a pat on the back, then fold both edges underneath the wings in half.

10 Fold the whole fuselage in half along the dotted line.

11 The fuselage is now ready, but you need now to add a tip to the nose in order to fire the Catapult Plane. This is very tricky and it can only be done if very thin paper is used in the folding.

The result after Step 6.

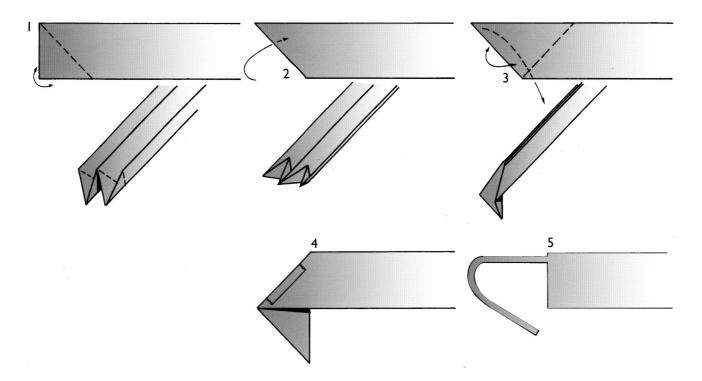

NOSE

1 & 2 Make inverted folds in the tip by folding backward and forward along the dotted line, then tuck in both tips.

3 Fold the resulting point backward and forward along the dotted line and push it down through the middle.

4 Secure the upper side of the nose with cellophane tape.

5 As we said, folding a nose hook is a tricky job; if you can do it, however, the final result is fantastic. Should the paper become so creased it's hard to make any kind of shape with it, the best thing to do is go back to Step 11, where the fuselage is complete. Now, your back-up is to simply twist open a paper clip and insert it into the nose, securing it with tape or glue. It's not perfect, but it can save blood, sweat and tears.

The Catapult Plane is fired with a rubber band. This can be done by stretching a rubber band between the thumb and the forefinger as shown and shooting the plane by the familiar "paper pellet" method. An even more effective way is to attach a rubber band to a small stick with strong tape.

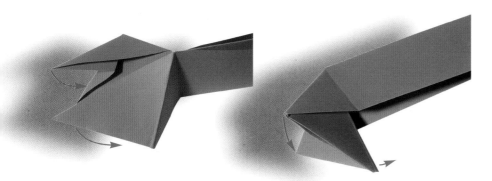

These models show the details of folding the paper nose hook, in case you prefer not to use a paper clip.

The striking look of the Flying Fish makes it very
special. Its shape combines the features of airplane
and fish—hence the name. The plane's flight
performance is extraordinary. It's easy to imagine it
leaping out of the water and being equally
at home in the air.
The method of construction is rather unusual: all
the folds are made first, then the Flying Fish is
shaped in a single action. If a face is painted on it,
the effect can be really startling.
The flight of the Flying Fish flight is quite unique and
achieved by having the elevator in the correct position:
which, unfortunately, takes a little practice.

*The Flying Fish is quite unique and
combines the features of an airplane
and a fish.*

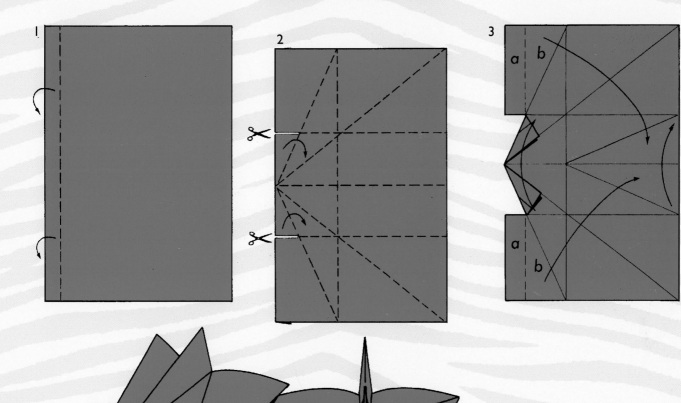

1 Take paper 8 X 12 inches (20 X 30cm), fold over a $^3/4$ inch (2cm) strip and fasten it down.

2 Make folds backward and forward along all these dotted lines. Doing this thoroughly will make the final folding easier. Make cuts in the places indicated on the left side, then fold over the resulting flaps and glue them down.

3 Now fold the entire form. Push the **b** triangles together, fold the tail as illustrated and staple or glue the **a** flaps together.

4. Here is what the model should look like underneath.

5 Like fighter planes in the Second World War, the Flying Fish would have a much more striking look with a face painted on it, as can be seen here.

Many people played with pea-shooters when they were kids. The Flying Arrow is made in much the same way as the traditional pea-shooter. It's best to make it using a page from a glossy magazine or even a comic book—although the latter are less successful. The expert paper airplane maker will simply rip out a rectangular sheet and quickly roll it up, giving the torn edge a good tongue licking, literally, as it reaches its final shape. The merging of the paper fibers glues the paper coils together quite effectively. Having made the fuselage, you add the tail section and the result is an excellent paper plane, although it is hard to believe just from looking at the picture.

The Flying Arrow is reminiscent of the old familiar paper arrow, and it flies beautifully.

FUSELAGE

1 Roll up a long strip of paper.

2 Keeping the paper rolled, stretch it out until you get a long point at one end. Secure the shape with cellophane tape.

WINGS

1 & 2 Take a sheet of paper 8 x 14 inches (20 x 35cm) and fold along the dotted lines. Push the points indicated by the arrows inward, so that the figure lies flat. This can be seen clearly in the diagram.

3 Fold the top layer of the tips of the wings into a vertical position.

4 Attach the lower side of the wing section to the fuselage with tape or, better still, some quick-drying glue. It may be necessary to cut a little off the end of the fuselage to provide the right angle, and a flat surface, to which to attach the wings.

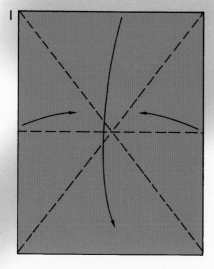

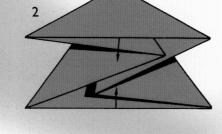

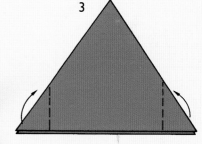

The model should be "launched" from a good height—don't just throw it! The top of a staircase is ideal. A really vertical throw—perhaps out of a window—suits the Flying Arrow best of all.

The Paper Helicopter is, in fact, a gyroplane
—the forerunner of the helicopter. It is very
easy to make and flies beautifully, spiralling
to the ground like the winged sycamore seed.

This is probably the easiest model to fold and yet its
performance is quite original and very effective. The
Paper Helicopter is another model from the *Scientific
American* International Airplane Competition and it
functions in the same way as a real helicopter.
Strictly speaking, it is a gyroplane, a forerunner of the
helicopter we know today. The gyroplane was
an airplane with small wings and freely rotating
overhead blades. The concept was abandoned when the
helicopter was invented.
When launched from a high place, our Paper Helicopter
can cover a distance of about a hundred yards
(or meters) using no power and with the rotary blades
operating just like those of a real helicopter.
As for it's future, who can tell? It may become a viable
commercial proposition as a reliable parachute design.
Although the gyroplane has been obsolete for over
thirty years, perhaps the popularity of this paper
model will imbue new life into it.

1 Take a sheet of paper 12 x 3
inches (30 x 7cm) and make cuts
in the three places indicated. Fold
the two resulting flaps on the left-
hand side along the dotted line—
one forward and one backward.
On the righthand side, fold the
edges in along the dotted lines,
then turn up the end.

2 Once the Paper Helicopter has
been glued or stapled together
it is ready for its maiden flight.
But remember to launch it from
as high a point as possible.

ANTI-AIRCRAFT DEVICE

The original idea for folding paper airplanes probably came from the childhood practice of launching paper pellets in the classroom. Paper airplanes provided a surer way of passing notes or other information—an aerodynamic skill needed less today due to the use of school computers and pocket e-mail.

Old-time paper pellets, however, can be made out of anything; size and paper type is unimportant, except that newspaper pellets, for some reason, are hard to shoot with a rubber band. You'll find here a new use for the traditional paper pellet and the Catapult Plane (pages 81–85) as defense weapons. The war game that follows is best played in a group. One side tries to fly as many paper airplanes as possible from A to B while the other side attempts to stop them from succeeding by shooting them down with pellets or the Catapult Plane.

A tiny paper pellet Anti-aircraft device makes an attack on a Sailplane.

Every airplane reaching B wins a point and every
airplane shot down is a point to the anti-aircraft team.
The larger the group playing, the more fun the game.
You also have to consider tactics. What is the best way
to defeat the enemy; should you fly in low over
the ground or stay as high as possible? Attack in force
or randomly? It's clear that a concealed battery of
pellet launchers can decimate large numbers of flying
airplanes at a time.
There are endless possibilities.

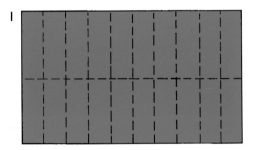

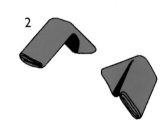

1 Roll-and-fold a strip of paper widthwise several times, then fold it in half.

2 The pellet should look like this. Now, stretch a rubber band between your thumb and forefinger as shown. With your other hand, fit the pellet around the middle of the band. Hold the paper pellet between the thumb and forefinger, and pull it backward. Then, hold, aim, and...fire!

The Catapult Plane is attacking the Hunter; which will crash first?

The Catapult Plane (pages 81–85) also performs well on defense. You can either shoot it by hand from the floor or use a sling. It's very satisfying to shoot a friend's paper airplane out of the sky.
The paper pellet is an anti-aircraft missile, but the Catapult Plane—although launched in a similar way—is closer to being a fighter plane. Make several, and prepare to do battle.

Creating new designs from standard models is fascinating—
it remains to be seen how many different designs can emerge
from one simple principle. In this case, you simply follow the
wing pattern for the Flying Arrow (pages 88–99) to make one
section of the Bomb. It's up to you how many sections to add,
depending on the size bomb you need. So far there's no
mention of it in the *Guinness Book of Records*.
The Bomb is an ideal deterrent to unwanted visitors. Drop it
from a high point, such as a window or the top of the stairs.

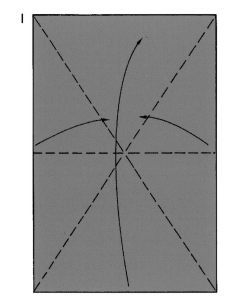

1 In a piece of paper 8 × 12 inches
(20 × 30cm) make folds along the
diagonals and through the center.

2 If you don't yet know the basic
method of folding it, see page 89
for instructions.

3 Fold the four sections along the
dotted lines.

4 Join two or more of these forms
together with glue or staples and
your Bomb is ready.

*The same basic principle is used for
both the Flying Arrow and the Bomb.*

INDEX

Proportional Paper Use Alternatives*
(in inches—sizes approximate)

Original	Alternatives
20 x 30cm	7 x 10.5
	8 x 12
	9 x 13.5
	10 x 15
25 x 30cm	8.5 x 10
	9.25 x 11
	10 x 12
	11.5 x 14
30 x 40cm	10.5 x 14
	12 x 16
	13.5 x 18
	15 x 20
16 x 30cm	5.5 x 11
	6 x 12
	7 x 14
	8.5 x 17
30 x 35cm	8.5 x 10
	9.5 x 11
	12 x 14
	14.5 x 17
20 x 40cm	5.5 x 11
	7 x 14
	8 x 16
	8.5 x 17
20 x 35cm	6.5 x 11
	7 x 12
	8 x 14
	9.75 x 17
30 x 7cm	10 x 2.5
	11 x 2.75
	12 x 3
	17 x 4.25

*Measurements of original models in centimeters. Alternatives provided to allow easier adjustment to paper sizes available. Models may or may not fly properly when constructed nonproportionally.